Mattt Thompson

NSHipster: Obscure Topics In Cocoa & Objective-C

Illustrated by Conor Heelan

ISBN 978-0-9912182-0-2

NSHipster
Portland, Oregon
http://nshipster.com

Table of Contents

Foundation & CoreFoundation 78

UIKit

Localization, Internationalization & Accessibility

API Design

Community 272

Introduction

To be an NSHipster is to care deeply about the craft of writing code. In cultivating a deep understanding and appreciation of Objective-C, its frameworks and ecosystem, one is able to create apps that delight and inspire users.

This book takes a structured approach to learning Objective-C development, starting from the language and system frameworks, and moving onto high-level concerns, like internationalization, design, and community. It is as much a technical manual as it is a meditation on the practice of coding.

I hope that by reading this, you will share in the excitement of discovering new insights, and taking pride in your work.

Objective-C

#pragma

#pragma declarations are a mark of craftsmanship in Objective-C. Although originally used to make source code portable across different compilers, the Xcode-savvy coder uses #pragma declarations to very different ends.

In this modern context, #pragma skirts the line between comment and code. As a preprocessor directive, #pragma evaluates at compile-time, but unlike other macros, #pragma is not used to change the runtime behavior of an application. Instead, #pragma declarations are used by Xcode to accomplish two primary tasks: organizing code and inhibiting compiler warnings.

Organizing Your Code

Code organization is a matter of hygiene. How you structure your code is a reflection on you and your work. A lack of convention and internal consistency indicates either carelessness or incompetence—and worse, makes a project difficult to maintain and collaborate on.

Good habits start with #pragma mark:

```objc
@implementation ViewController
- (id)init {
    ...
}
#pragma mark - UIViewController
- (void)viewDidLoad {
    ...
}
#pragma mark - IBAction
- (IBAction)cancel:(id)sender {
    ...
}
#pragma mark - UITableViewDataSource
- (NSInteger)tableView:(UITableView *)tableView
numberOfRowsInSection:(NSInteger)section
{

}
#pragma mark - UITableViewDelegate
- (void)tableView:(UITableView *)tableView
didSelectRowAtIndexPath:(NSIndexPath *)indexPath {
    ...
}
```

Use #pragma mark in your @implementation to divide code into logical sections. Not only do these sections make it easier to read through the code itself, but it also adds visual cues to the Xcode source navigator.

#pragma mark declarations starting with a dash (-) are preceded with a horizontal divider.

Start by grouping methods according to their originating class. For example, an NSInputStream subclass would have a group marked NSInputStream, followed by a group marked NSStream.

Things like IBAction outlets, or methods corresponding to target / action, notification, or KVO selectors probably deserve their own sections as well.

Finally, if a class conforms to any @protocols, group all of the methods from each protocol together, and add a #pragma mark header with the name of that protocol.

Your code should be clean enough to eat off of. So take the time to leave your .m files better than how you found them.

Inhibiting Warnings

What's even more annoying than poorly-formatted code? Code that generates warnings. *Especially 3rd-party code.* There are few things as irksome as that one vendor library that takes forever to compile, and finishes with 200+ warnings. Even shipping code with a single warning is in poor form.

Try setting the -Weverything flag and checking the "Treat Warnings as Errors" box your build settings.
This turns on Hard Mode in Xcode.

But sometimes there's no avoiding compiler warnings. Deprecation notices and retain-cycle false positives are two common examples where this might happen. In those rare cases where you are *absolutely certain* that a particular compiler warning should be inhibited, #pragma can be used to suppress them:

```
#pragma clang diagnostic push
#pragma clang diagnostic ignored "-Wunused-variable"
    OSStatus status = SecItemExport(...);
    NSCAssert(status == errSecSuccess, @"%d", status);
#pragma clang diagnostic pop
```

This code sample is an example of an otherwise unavoidable warning from the static analyzer. When compiling in Release mode, assertions are ignored, so Clang warns that status is an unused variable.

Using #pragma clang diagnostic push/pop, you can tell the compiler to ignore certain warnings for a particular section of code (the original diagnostic settings are restored with the final pop).

Just don't use #pragma as a way to sweep legitimate warnings under the rug—it will only come back to bite you later.

You can read more about the LLVM's use of #pragma in the Clang Compiler User's Manual.

Like a thrift store 8-track player turned into that lamp in the foyer, #pragma remains a curious vestige of the past: Once the secret language of compilers, it is now re-purposed to better-communicate intent to other programmers.

How delightfully vintage!

nil / Nil / NULL / NSNull

Understanding the concept of nothingness is as much a philosophical issue as it is a pragmatic one. We are inhabitants of a universe made up of *somethings*, yet reason in a logical universe with existential uncertainties. As a physical manifestation of a logical system, computers are faced with the intractable problem of how to represent *nothing* with *something*.

In Objective-C, there are several different varieties of nothing.

C represents nothing as 0 for primitive values, and NULL for pointers (which is equivalent to 0 in a pointer context).

Objective-C builds on C's representation of nothing by adding nil. nil is an object pointer to nothing. Although semantically distinct from NULL, they are equivalent to one another.

On the framework level, Foundation defines the NSNull class, which defines a single class method, +null, which returns a singleton NSNull instance. NSNull is different from nil or NULL, in that it is an actual object, rather than a zero value.

Additionally, in Foundation/NSObjCRuntime.h, Nil is defined as a class pointer to nothing. This lesser-known title-case cousin of nil doesn't show up much very often, but it's at least worth noting.

There's Something About nil

Newly-alloc'd NSObjects start life with their contents set to 0. This means that all pointers an object has to other objects begin as nil, so it's unnecessary to, for instance, set self.association = nil in init methods.

Perhaps the most notable behavior of nil, though, is that it handles messages sent to it.

In other languages, like C++, sending a message to a null pointer would crash a program, but in Objective-C, invoking a method on nil returns a zero value. This greatly simplifies expressions, as it obviates the need to check for nil before doing anything:

```
// For example, this expression...
if (name != nil && [name isEqualToString:@"Steve"])
{ ... }

// ...can be simplified to:
if ([name isEqualToString:@"steve"]) { ... }
```

Being aware of how nil works in Objective-C allows this convenience to be a feature, rather than a source of hard-to-find bugs.

Guard against cases where nil values are unwanted, either by returning early, or adding a NSParameterAssert to throw an exception.

NSNull: Something for Nothing

NSNull is used throughout Foundation and other system frameworks to skirt around the limitations of collections like NSArray and NSDictionary, which cannot contain nil values. NSNull effectively boxes NULL or nil values, so that they can be stored in collections:

```
NSMutableDictionary *mutableDictionary =
[NSMutableDictionary dictionary];

mutableDictionary[@"someKey"] = [NSNull null];
// Sets value of NSNull singleton for `someKey`

NSLog(@"Keys: %@", [mutableDictionary allKeys]);
// @[@"someKey"]
```

So to recap, here are the four values representing nothing that every Objective-C programmer should know about:

Symbol	Value	Meaning
NULL	(void *)0	literal null value for C pointers
nil	(id)0	literal null value for Objective-C objects
Nil	(Class)0	literal null value for Objective-C classes
NSNull	[NSNull null]	singleton object used to represent null

BOOL / bool / Boolean / NSCFBoolean

Truth, *Vēritās*: The entire charter of Philosophy is founded upon the pursuit of it, and yet its exact meaning and implications still elude us.

Does truth exist independently, or is it defined contingently?
Can a proposition be at once both true and false?
Is there absolute truth in anything, or is everything relative?

Once again, encoding our logical universe into the cold, calculating bytecode of computers forces us to deal with these questions one way or another. And as you'll see from our discussion of boolean types in C & Objective-C, truth is indeed stranger than fiction.

Objective-C defines BOOL to encode truth value. It is a typedef of a signed char, with the macros YES and NO to represent true and false, respectively.

Boolean values are used in conditionals, such as if or while statements, to conditionally perform logic or repeat execution. When evaluating a conditional statement, the value 0 is considered "false", while any other value is considered "true". Because NULL and nil have a value of 0, they are considered "false" as well.

In Objective-C, use the BOOL type for parameters, properties, and instance variables dealing with truth values. When assigning literal values, use the YES and NO macros.

The Wrong Answer to the Wrong Question

Novice programmers often include an equality operator when evaluating conditionals:

```
if ([a isEqual:b] == YES) { ... }
```

Not only is this unnecessary, but depending on the left-hand value, it may also lead to unexpected results. Consider this function, which returns whether two integers are different:

```
static BOOL different (int a, int b) {
    return a - b;
}
```

A programmer might take some satisfaction in the clever simplicity of this approach: indeed, two integers are equal if and only if their difference is 0.

However, because BOOL is typedef'd as a signed char on 32-bit architectures, this will not behave as expected:

```
different(11, 10) // YES
different(10, 11) // NO (!)
different(512, 256) // NO (!)
```

Now, this might be acceptable for JavaScript, but Objective-C don't suffer fools gladly.

On a 64-bit iOS, BOOL is defined as a bool, rather than signed char, which precludes the runtime from these type conversion errors.

Deriving truth value directly from an arithmetic operation is never a good idea. Use the == operator, or cast values into booleans with the ! (or !!) operator.

The Truth About NSNumber and BOOL

Pop quiz: what is the output of the following expression?

```
NSLog(@"%@", [@(YES) class]);
```

The answer:

```
__NSCFBoolean
```

Wait, what?

All this time, we've been led to believe that NSNumber boxes primitives into an object representation. Any other integer or float derived NSNumber object shows its class to be __NSCFNumber. What gives?

NSCFBoolean is a private class in the NSNumber class cluster. It is a bridge to the CFBooleanRef type, which is used to wrap boolean values for Core Foundation collections and property lists. CFBoolean defines the constants kCFBooleanTrue and kCFBooleanFalse. Because CFNumberRef and CFBooleanRef are different types in Core Foundation, it makes sense that they are represented by different bridging classes in NSNumber.

Wrapping things up, here is a table with the truth types and values in Objective-C:

Name	Type	Header	True	False
BOOL	signed char / bool	objc.h	YES	NO
bool	_Bool (int)	stdbool.h	TRUE	FALSE
Boolean	unsigned char	MacTypes.h	TRUE	FALSE
NSNumber	__NSCFBoolean	Foundation.h	@(YES)	@(NO)

Equality

The concept of equality is a central point of debate and inquiry in philosophy and mathematics, with far-reaching implications for matters of ethics, justice, and public policy.

From an empiricist perspective of the universe, two objects are equal if they are indistinguishable from one another in measurable observations. Egalitarians, operating on a human scale, hold that individuals should be considered equal members of the societal, economic, political, and judicial systems they inhabit.

It is the task of programmers to reconcile our logical and physical understanding of equality with the semantic domains we model.

Equality & Identity

First and foremost, it is important to make a distinction between *equality* and *identity*.

Two objects may be equal or equivalent to one another, if they share a common set of properties. Yet, those two objects may still be thought to be distinct, each with their own identity.

In code, an object's identity is tied to its memory address.

NSObject tests equality with another object with the method isEqual:. In its base implementation, an equality check is essentially a test for identity:

```
@implementation NSObject (Approximate)
- (BOOL)isEqual:(id)object {
  return self == object;
}
@end
```

isEqual

Subclasses of NSObject implementing their own isEqual: method are expected to do the following:

- Implement a new isEqualTo*ClassName*: method, which performs the meaningful value comparison.

- Override isEqual: to make class and object identity checks, falling back on the aforementioned class comparison method.

- Override hash, which will be described in the next section.

For container classes like NSArray, NSDictionary, and NSString, equality deep equality comparison, testing equality for each member in pairwise fashion:

```
@implementation NSArray (Approximate)
- (BOOL)isEqualToArray:(NSArray *)array {
  if (!array || [self count] != [array count]) {
    return NO;
  }

  for (NSUInteger idx = 0; idx < [array count]; idx++) {
      if (![self[idx] isEqual:array[idx]]) {
          return NO;
      }
  }

  return YES;
}

- (BOOL)isEqual:(id)object {
  if (self == object) {
    return YES;
  }

  if (![object isKindOfClass:[NSArray class]]) {
    return NO;
  }

  return [self isEqualToArray:(NSArray *)object];
}
@end
```

isEqualTo____:

The following NSObject subclasses in Foundation have custom equality implementations, with the corresponding method:

NSAttributedString	-isEqualToAttributedString:
NSData	-isEqualToData:
NSDate	-isEqualToDate:
NSDictionary	-isEqualToDictionary:
NSHashTable	-isEqualToHashTable:
NSIndexSet	-isEqualToIndexSet:
NSNumber	-isEqualToNumber:
NSOrderedSet	-isEqualToOrderedSet:
NSSet	-isEqualToSet:
NSString	-isEqualToString:
NSTimeZone	-isEqualToTimeZone:
NSValue	-isEqualToValue:

When comparing two instances of any of these classes, one is encouraged to use these high-level methods rather than isEqual:.

However, our theoretical implementation is yet incomplete. Let's turn our attention now to hash, after a quick detour to clear something up about NSString.

The Curious Case of NSString Equality

As an interesting aside, consider the following:

```
NSString *a = @"Hello";
NSString *b = @"Hello";
BOOL wtf = (a == b); // YES (!)
```

To be perfectly clear: the correct way to compare two NSString objects is -isEqualToString:. Under no circumstances should NSString objects be compared with the == operator.

So what's going on here? Why does this work, when the same code for NSArray or NSDictionary literals wouldn't do this?

It all has to do with an optimization technique known as string interning, whereby one copy of immutable string values. NSString *a and *b point to the same copy of the interned string value @"Hello".

Again, this only works for statically-defined, immutable strings. Constructing identical strings with NSString +stringWithFormat: will objects with different pointers.

Interestingly enough, Objective-C selector names are also stored as interned strings in a shared string pool.

Hashing

The primary use case of object equality tests for object-oriented programming is to determine collection membership. To keep this fast, subclasses with custom equality implementations are expected to implement hash:

- Object equality is commutative
  ([a isEqual:b] $\Rightarrow$ [b isEqual:a])

- If objects are equal, their hash values must also be equal
  ([a isEqual:b] $\Rightarrow$ [a hash] == [b hash])

- However, the converse does not hold: two objects need not be equal in order for their hash values to be equal
  ([a hash] == [b hash] $\neg\Rightarrow$ [a isEqual:b])

Now for a quick flashback to Computer Science 101:

Hashing Fundamentals

A hash table is a fundamental data structure in programming, and it's what enables NSSet & NSDictionary to have fast ($O(1)$) lookup of elements.

We can best understand hash tables by contrasting them to arrays.

Arrays store elements in sequential indexes, such that an Array of size n will have slots at positions 0, 1, up to n - 1. To determine where an element is stored in the array (if at all), each position would have to be checked one-by-one (unless the array happens to be sorted, but that's another story).

Hash Tables take a slightly different approach. Rather than storing elements sequentially (0, 1, ..., n-1), a hash table allocates n positions in memory, and uses a function to calculate a position within that range.

A hash function is deterministic, and a good hash function generates values in a relatively uniform distribution without being too computationally expensive. A hash collision occurs when two different objects calculate the same hash value. When this happens, the hash table will seek from the point of collision and place the new object in the first open slot. As a hash table becomes more congested, the likelihood of collision increases, which leads to more time spent looking for a free space.

One of the most common misconceptions about implementing a custom hash function is that hash values must be distinct. This often leads to needlessly complicated implementations, with incantations copied from Java textbooks. In reality, a simple XOR over the hash values of critical properties is sufficient most of the time.

The trick is in determining the critical values of an object.

For an NSDate, the time interval since a reference date would be enough to go on:

```
@implementation NSDate (Approximate)
- (NSUInteger)hash {
    return abs([self timeIntervalSinceReferenceDate]);
}
```

For a UIColor, a bit-shifted sum of RGB components would be a convenient calculation:

```
@implementation UIColor (Approximate)
- (NSUInteger)hash {
    CGFloat red, green, blue;
    [self getRed:&red green:&green blue:&blue alpha:nil];
    return ((NSUInteger)(red * 255) << 16) +
           ((NSUInteger)(green * 255) << 8) +
            (NSUInteger)(blue * 255);
}
@end
```

Implementing -isEqual: and hash in a Subclass

Bringing it all together, here's how one might override the default equality implementation for a subclass:

Person.h

```
@interface Person
@property NSString *name;
@property NSDate *birthday;

- (BOOL)isEqualToPerson:(Person *)person;
@end
```

Person.m

```
@implementation Person
- (BOOL)isEqualToPerson:(Person *)person {
  if (!person) {
    return NO;
  }

  BOOL haveEqualNames = (!self.name && !person.name) ||
      [self.name isEqualToString:person.name];

  BOOL haveEqualBirthdays =
      (!self.birthday && !person.birthday) ||
      [self.birthday isEqualToDate:person.birthday];

  return haveEqualNames && haveEqualBirthdays;
}
```

```
#pragma mark - NSObject

- (BOOL)isEqual:(id)object {
  if (self == object) {
    return YES;
  }

  if (![object isKindOfClass:[Person class]]) {
    return NO;
  }

  return [self isEqualToPerson:(Person *)object];
}
- (NSUInteger)hash {
  return [self.name hash] ^ [self.birthday hash];
}
@end
```

Don't Overthink It

While all of this has been an interesting exercise in epistemology and computer science, there is one lingering pragmatic detail:

You don't usually need to implement this.

There are many situations where the default identity check (two variables point to the same address in memory) is indeed desirable behavior. Such is a consequence of data modeling being inherently limited.

Take, for instance, the previous example of the Person class. It's not inconceivable that two individuals would share a common name and birthday. In reality, this crisis of identity would be resolved by additional information, whether it's a system-dependent identifier like a Social Security Number, their parents' identities, or any other physical attributes.

Ultimately, it's up to the abstraction to isolate the significant, identifying features that the system cares about, and disregard the rest.

Hopefully, after all of this explanation, we all stand with equal footing on this slippery subject.

As humans, we strive to understand and implement equality in our society and economy; in the laws and leaders that govern us; in the understanding that we extend to one another as we journey through existence. May we continue towards that ideal, where an individual is judged by the contents of their character, just as we judge a variable by the contents of its memory address.

Type Encodings

Number stations, numerology, hieroglyphs, hobo codes; there is something truly fascinating about information that hides in plain sight. Though hidden messages are rarely useful or particularly interesting in and of themselves, it's the thrill of the hunt that piques our deepest curiosities.

The secret codes of Objective-C are Type Encodings.

@encode, one of the @ Compiler Directives, returns a C string that encodes the internal representation of a given type, for example, @encode(int) → i. This is similar to the ANSI C typeof operator.

Apple's Objective-C runtime uses type encodings internally to help facilitate message dispatching.

Here's a rundown of the Objective-C Type Encodings:

Code	Meaning
c	A char
i	An int
s	A short
l	A longl is treated as a 32-bit quantity on 64-bit programs.
q	A long long
C	An unsigned char
I	An unsigned int
S	An unsigned short
L	An unsigned long
Q	An unsigned long long
f	A float
d	A double
B	A C++ bool or a C99 _Bool
v	A void
*	A character string (char *)
@	An object (whether statically typed or typed id)
#	A class object (Class)
:	A method selector (SEL)
[array type]	An array
{name=type...}	A structure
(name=type...)	A union
bnum	A bit field of num bits
^type	A pointer to type
?	An unknown type (among other things, this code is used for function pointers)

Of course, charts are fine, but experimenting in code is even better:

```
NSLog(@"int        : %s", @encode(int));
NSLog(@"float      : %s", @encode(float));
NSLog(@"float *    : %s", @encode(float*));
NSLog(@"char       : %s", @encode(char));
NSLog(@"char *     : %s", @encode(char *));
NSLog(@"BOOL       : %s", @encode(BOOL));
NSLog(@"void       : %s", @encode(void));
NSLog(@"void *     : %s", @encode(void *));

NSLog(@"NSObject * : %s", @encode(NSObject *));
NSLog(@"NSObject   : %s", @encode(NSObject));
NSLog(@"[NSObject] : %s", @encode(typeof([NSObject
class])));
NSLog(@"NSError ** : %s", @encode(typeof(NSError **)));

int intArray[5] = {1, 2, 3, 4, 5};
NSLog(@"int[]      : %s", @encode(typeof(intArray)));

float floatArray[3] = {0.1f, 0.2f, 0.3f};
NSLog(@"float[]    : %s", @encode(typeof(floatArray)));

typedef struct _struct {
    short a;
    long long b;
    unsigned long long c;
} Struct;
NSLog(@"struct     : %s", @encode(typeof(Struct)));
```

Result:

```
int        : i
float      : f
float *    : ^f
char       : c
char *     : *
BOOL       : c
void       : v
void *     : ^v

NSObject * : @
NSObject   : #
[NSObject] : {NSObject=#}
NSError ** : ^@

int[]      : [5i]
float[]    : [3f]
struct     : {_struct=sqQ}
```

There are some interesting takeaways from this:

- Whereas the standard encoding for pointers is a preceding ^, char * gets its own code: *. This makes sense conceptually, since C strings are thought to be entities in and of themselves, rather than a pointer to something else.

- BOOL is c, rather than i, as one might expect. Reason being, char is smaller than an int, and when Objective-C was originally designed in the 80's, bits (much like the US Dollar) were more valuable than they are today.

- Passing NSObject directly yields #. However, passing [NSObject class] yields a struct named NSObject with a single class field. That is, of course, the isa field, which all NSObject instances have to signify their type.

Method Encodings

As mentioned in Apple's "Objective-C Runtime Programming Guide", there are a handful of type encodings that are used internally, but cannot be returned with @encode.

These are the type qualifiers for methods declared in a protocol:

Code	Meaning
r	const
n	in
N	inout
o	out
O	bycopy
R	byref
V	oneway

Anyone familiar with NSDistantObject should recognize these as a vestige of Distributed Objects.

Although it has fallen out of fashion in the age of iOS, DO is an interprocess messaging protocol used to communicate between Cocoa applications. Under these constraints, there were benefits to be had from the additional context.

By default, parameters in distributed object messages were passed as proxies, except in situations where proxying would be unnecessarily inefficient; the bycopy qualifier could be specified to make sure a full copy of the object was sent instead.

Parameters were also inout by default, signifying that objects needed to be sent back and forth when sending the message. By specifying a parameter as just in or out instead, the application could avoid the round-trip overhead.

So what do we gain from our newfound understanding of Objective-C Type Encodings? Honestly, not that much.

But as we said from the very outset, there is wisdom in the pursuit of deciphering secret messages. Looking at type encodings reveals details about Objective-C runtime internals, which is a noble pursuit in and of itself.

C Storage Classes

In C, the scope and lifetime of a variable or function is determined by its storage class. Each variable has a lifetime, or the context in which they store their value. Functions, along with variables, also exist within a particular scope, or visibility, which dictates which parts of a program know about them.

There are 4 storage classes in C: auto, register, static & extern.

auto

There's a good chance you've never seen this keyword in the wild. That's because auto is the default storage class, and therefore rarely needs to be specified explicitly.

Automatic variables have memory automatically allocated when a program enters a block, and released when the program leaves that block. Access to automatic variables is limited to only the block in which they are declared, as well as any nested blocks.

register

Most Objective-C programmers probably aren't familiar with register either, as it's not widely used in the NS world.

register behaves just like auto, except that instead of being allocated onto the stack, they are stored in a register.

Registers offer faster access than RAM, but because of the complexities of memory management, putting variables in registers does not always guarantee a faster program—in fact, it may very well end up slowing down execution by taking up space on the register unnecessarily. As it were, using register is no more than a mere suggestion to the compiler; implementations may choose whether or not to honor this.

register's lack of popularity in Objective-C is instructive: it's probably best not to bother with. It will sooner cause a headache than any noticeable speedup.

static

Finally, one that everyone's sure to recognize: static.

As a keyword, static gets used in a lot of different ways, so it can be confusing to figure out exactly what it means in every instance. When it comes to storage classes, static means one of two things.

1. A static variable inside a method or function retains its value between invocations.

2. A static variable declared globally can called by any function or method, so long as those functions appear in the same file as the static variable. The same goes for static functions.

Static Singletons

A common pattern in Objective-C is the static singleton, wherein a statically-declared variable is initialized and returned in either a function or class method:

```
+ (instancetype)sharedInstance {
  static id _sharedInstance = nil;
  static dispatch_once_t onceToken;
  dispatch_once(&onceToken, ^{
      _sharedInstance = [[self alloc] init];
      // any further configuration
  });

  return _sharedInstance;
}
```

The singleton pattern is useful for creating objects that are shared across the entire application, such as a notification manager, or objects that may be expensive to create, such as date formatters.

extern

Whereas static makes functions and variables globally visible within a particular file, extern makes them visible globally to all files.

Global variables are not a great idea, generally speaking. Having no constraints on how or when state can be mutated is just asking for impossible-to-debug situations.

That said, there are two common and practical uses for extern in Objective-C: constants and public functions.

Global String Constants

Any time your application uses a string constant in a public interface, it should be declared as an external string constant. This is especially true of NSNotification names, NSError domains, and keys in userInfo dictionaries.

Declare an extern NSString * const in a public header, and define that NSString * const in the implementation:

AppDelegate.h

```
extern NSString * const kAppErrorDomain;
```

AppDelegate.m

```objc
NSString * const kAppErrorDomain =
@"com.example.yourapp.error";
```

It doesn't particularly matter what the value of the string is, so long as it's unique.

Public Functions

Some APIs may wish to expose helper functions publicly. The pattern follows the same as in the previous example:

TransactionStateMachine.h

```objc
typedef NS_ENUM(NSUInteger, TransactionState) {
    TransactionOpened,
    TransactionPending,
    TransactionClosed,
};

extern NSString *
  NSStringFromTransactionState(TransactionState state);
```

TransactionStateMachine.m

```
NSString *
  NSStringFromTransactionState(TransactionState state) {
  switch (state) {
    case TransactionOpened:      return @"Opened"
    case TransactionPending:     return @"Pending";
    case TransactionClosed:      return @"Closed";
    default:                     return nil;
  }
}
```

To understand anything is to make sense of its context. What we may see as obvious and self-evident, is all but unknown to someone outside our frame of reference. Our inability to truly understand or appreciate the differences in perspective between ourselves and others is perhaps our most basic shortcoming.

That is why, in our constructed logical universe of 0's and 1's, we take such care to separate contexts, and structure our assumptions based on these explicit rules. C storage classes are essential to understanding how a program operates. Take heed of these simple rules of engagement and go forth to code with confidence.

@

Birdwatchers refer to it as "Jizz": those indefinable characteristics unique to a particular kind of thing.

This term can be appropriated to describe how seasoned individuals might distinguish Rust from Go, or Ruby from Elixir at a glance. Some just stick out like sore thumbs:

Perl, with all of its short variable names and special characters, reads like Q*bert swearing.

Lisp's profusion of parentheses is best captured by that old joke about a computer science student proving that they actually finished their homework by showing the last page:

```
        )))))
         )))
      ))
    )))) ))
  )))) ))
 )))
)
```

So if one were to go code-watching for the elusive Objective-C species, what would we look for?

- Square brackets
- Ridiculously-long method names
- @'s

@, or "at" sign compiler directives, are as central to understanding Objective-C's gestalt as its ancestry and infrastructure. It's the sugary glue that allows Objective-C to be such a powerful, expressive language, and yet still compile all the way down to C.

Its uses are varied and disparate, such that the only way to accurately describe what @ means by itself is "shorthand for something to do with Objective-C". @ compiler directives cover a broad range in usefulness and obscurity, with staples like @interface and @implementation, as well as ones a developer go their whole career without running into, like @defs and @compatibility_alias.

But to anyone aspiring to be an NSHipster, intimate familiarity with @ directives is tantamount to a music lover's ability to list all of The Beatles albums in chronological order (and most importantly, having unreasonably strong opinions about each of them).

Interface & Implementation

@interface and @implementation are the first things you learn about when you start Objective-C:

- @interface...@end

- @implementation...@end

What you don't learn about until later on, are categories and class extensions.

Categories allow you to extend the behavior of existing classes by adding new methods. As a convention, categories are defined in their own .{h,m} files, like so:

MyObject+CategoryName.h

```
@interface MyObject (CategoryName)
  + (BOOL)barWithBaz:(NSInteger)baz;
  - (void)foo;
@end
```

MyObject+CategoryName.m

```objc
@implementation MyObject (CategoryName)
  + (BOOL)barWithBaz:(NSInteger)baz {
    return baz < 42;
  }

  - (void)foo {
    // ...
  }
@end
```

Categories are particularly useful for convenience methods on standard framework classes (just don't go overboard with your utility functions).

Rather than littering your code with random, arbitrary color values, create an NSColor / UIColor category that defines class methods like +appNameDarkGrayColor. You can then add a semantic layer on top of that by creating method aliases like +appNameTextColor, which returns +appNameDarkGrayColor.

Extensions look like categories, but omit the category name. These are typically declared in the .m file before an @implementation to specify a private interface, and even override properties declared in the original @interface:

MyObject.m

```
@interface MyObject ()
@property (readwrite, nonatomic, strong) NSString *name;
- (void)doSomething;
@end

@implementation MyObject
// ...
@end
```

Properties

Property directives are also learned early on:

- @property
- @synthesize
- @dynamic

As of Xcode 4.4, it is no longer necessary to explicitly synthesize properties. Properties declared in an @interface are automatically synthesized in the implementation with leading underscore ivar name, i.e. @synthesize property = _property.

Forward Class Declarations

Occasionally, @interface declarations will reference an external class in a property or as a parameter type. Rather than adding #import statements for each class, it's good practice to use forward class declarations in the header, and import them in the implementation.

- @class

Shorter compile times, less clutter, reduced chance of cyclical references; you should definitely get in the habit of doing this if you aren't already.

Instance Variable Visibility

As a matter of general convention, classes provide accessor and mutator interfaces through properties and methods, rather than directly exposing ivars.

Although ARC makes working with ivars much safer, the aforementioned automatic property synthesis removes the one place where ivars would otherwise be declared.

Nonetheless, to accommodate cases where ivars must be directly manipulated, there are the following visibility directives:

- @public: instance variable can be read and written to directly, using the notation person->age = 32"

- @package: instance variable is public, except outside of the framework in which it is specified (64-bit architectures only)

- @protected: instance variable is only accessible to its class and derived classes

- @private: instance variable is only accessible to its class

---

Person.h

```
@interface Person : NSObject {
  @public
  NSString name;
  int age;

  @private
  int salary;
}
```

Protocols

There's a critical point in an Objective-C programmer's evolution, when one realizes that they can define their own protocols.

The beauty of protocols is that they allow programmers to create loosely-coupled APIs.

It's the egalitarian mantra at the heart of the American Dream: that it doesn't matter who you are, or where you come from: anyone can achieve anything if they work hard enough.

...or at least that's idea, right?

- @protocol...@end: Defines a set of methods to be implemented by any class conforming to the protocol, as if they were added to the interface of that class.

Requirement Options

You can further tailor a protocol by specifying methods as required or optional. Optional methods are stubbed in the interface, but do not generate a warning if the method is not implemented. Protocol methods are required by default.

The syntax for @required and @optional follows that of the visibility macros:

CustomControlDelegate.h

```
@protocol CustomControlDelegate
    - (void)control:(CustomControl *)control
didSucceedWithResult:(id)result;

@optional
    - (void)control:(CustomControl *)control
    didFailWithError:(NSError *)error;
@end
```

Exception Handling

Objective-C communicates unexpected state primarily through NSError. Whereas other languages would use exception handling for this, Objective-C relegates exceptions to truly exceptional behavior, such as programmer error.

@ directives are used for the traditional convention of try/catch/finally blocks:

```
@try{
    // attempt to execute the following statements
    [self getValue:&value error:&error];

    // if an exception is raised, or explicitly thrown...
    if (error) {
      @throw exception;
    }
} @catch(NSException *e) {
    // ...handle the exception here
}  @finally {
    // always execute this at the end of either the @try
or @catch block
    [self cleanup];
}
```

Literals

Literals are shorthand notation for specifying fixed values. As a language feature, their existence is directly correlated with programmer happiness. By this measure, Objective-C has long been a language of programmer misery.

Object Literals

Until recently, Objective-C only had object literals for NSString. But with the release of the Apple LLVM 4.0 compiler, literals for NSNumber, NSArray and NSDictionary were added. And there was much rejoicing.

- @"Hello": Returns an NSString object initialized with the Unicode content inside the quotation marks.

- @42, @3.14, @YES, @'Z': Returns an NSNumber object initialized with pertinent class constructor, such that

  @42 → [NSNumber numberWithInteger:42], or

  @YES → [NSNumber numberWithBool:YES], or with suffixes to further specify type, like

  @42U → [NSNumber numberWithUnsignedInt:42U].

- @[]: Returns an NSArray object initialized with the comma-delimited list of objects as its contents.

For example, @[@"A", @NO, @2.718] →
[NSArray arrayWithObjects:@"A", @NO, @2.718, nil]
(Note that sentinel nil is not required in the literal).

- @{}: Returns an NSDictionary object initialized with the
  specified key-value pairs as its contents, in the format:
  @{@"someKey" : @"theValue"}.

- @(): Dynamically evaluates the boxed expression and
  returns the appropriate object literal based on its value
  (i.e. NSString for const char*, NSNumber for int, etc.).
  This is also the designated way to use number literals with
  enum values.

Objective-C Literals

Although it's uncommon, selectors and protocols can be
passed as method parameters. @selector() and @protocol()
serve as pseudo-literal directives that return a pointer to a
particular selector (SEL) or protocol (Protocol *).

- @selector(): Returns an SEL pointer to a selector with the
  specified name.
  Used in methods like -performSelector:withObject:.

- @protocol(): Returns a Protocol * pointer to the protocol
  with the specified name.
  Used in methods like -conformsToProtocol:.

C Literals

@ directives can also work the other way around, transforming Objective-C objects into C values. These ones in particular allow a peek underneath the Objective-C veil, to begin to understand what's really going on.

Did you know that all Objective-C classes and objects are just glorified structs? Or that the entire identity of an object hinges on a single field in that struct?

For most of us, coming into this knowledge is but an academic exercise. But for anyone venturing into low-level optimizations, this is simply the jumping-off point.

- @encode(): Returns the type encoding of a type. This type value can be used as the first argument encode in NSCoder -encodeValueOfObjCType:at.

- @defs(): Returns the layout of an Objective-C class. For example, to declare a struct with the same fields as an NSObject, you would simply do:

```
struct {
  @defs(NSObject)
}
```

@defs is unavailable in the modern Objective-C runtime.

Optimizations

There are two @ compiler directives specifically purposed for providing shortcuts for common optimizations.

- @autoreleasepool{}: If your code contains a tight loop that creates lots of temporary objects, you can use the @autorelease directive to optimize by being more aggressive about how for these short-lived, locally-scoped objects are deallocated. @autoreleasepool replaces and improves upon the old NSAutoreleasePool, which is significantly slower, and unavailable with ARC.

- @synchronized(){}: This directive offers a convenient way to guarantee safe execution of a particular code block within a specified context (usually self). Locking in this way is expensive, however, so for classes aiming for a particular level of thread safety, a dedicated NSLock property or the use of low-level locking functions like OSAtomicCompareAndSwap32(3) are recommended.

Compatibility

Rounding out the list of @ directives is the most esoteric of all:

- @compatibility_alias: Allows existing classes to be aliased by a different name.

@compatibility_alias can be used to significantly improve the experience of working with classes across major OS versions, allowing developers to back-port their own custom implementations of new functionality, without changing how that class is used in the app.

@ is a versatile, power-packed character, that embodies the underlying design and mechanisms of Objective-C. Knowing its many uses is key to getting at the best parts of the language.

__attribute__

Like any craft, one's effectiveness as a practitioner is contingent on how they treat their tools. Take good care of them, and they'll take good care of you.

Of all of the tools on a programmer's workbench, there is none more vital or powerful than the compiler.

__attribute__ is a compiler directive that specifies characteristics on declarations. They allow the compiler to perform advanced optimizations and enable new kinds of warnings for the analyzer.

The syntax for this keyword is __attribute__ followed by two sets of parentheses. __attribute__ directives are placed after function, variable, and type declarations. Inside the parentheses is a comma-delimited list of attributes.

```
// Return the square of a number
int square(int n) __attribute__((const));


// Declare the availability of a particular API
void f(void)
__attribute__((availability(macosx,introduced=10.4,depre
cated=10.6)));


// Send printf-like message to stderr and exit
extern void die(const char *format, ...)
    __attribute__((noreturn, format(printf, 1, 2)));
```

The double parentheses makes it easy to "macro out", especially with multiple attributes.

If this reminds you of ISO C's #pragma, you're not alone.

In fact, when __attribute__ was first introduced to GCC, it was faced with some resistance by some who suggested that #pragma be used exclusively for the same purposes.

There are, however, two very good reasons why __attribute__ exists:

1. It is impossible to generate #pragma commands from a macro.

2. There is no telling what the same #pragma might mean in another compiler.

Quoth the GCC Documentation for Function Attributes:

These two reasons applied to almost any application that might have been proposed for #pragma. It was basically a mistake to use #pragma for anything.

Indeed, if you look at modern Objective-C—in the headers of Apple frameworks and well-engineered open-source projects —__attribute__ is used for myriad purposes.

GCC

format

The format attribute specifies that a function takes format arguments in the style of printf, scanf, strftime or strfmon.

```
extern int
my_printf (void *my_object, const char *my_format, ...)
  __attribute__((format(printf, 2, 3)));
```

Objective-C programmers can also use the __NSString__ format to enforce the same rules as format strings in NSLog() NSString +stringWithFormat:.

nonnull

The nonnull attribute specifies that some function parameters should be non-null pointers.

```
extern void *
my_memcpy (void *dest, const void *src, size_t len)
  __attribute__((nonnull (1, 2)));
```

Using nonnull codifies expectations about values into an explicit contract, which can help catch any NULL pointer bugs lurking in any calling code.

Compile-time errors » run-time errors.

---

noreturn

A few standard library functions, such as abort and exit, cannot return. GCC knows this automatically. The noreturn attribute specifies this for any other function that don't return.

For instance, a method could specify the noreturn attribute for a thread entry point method, used when spawning a dedicated NSThread, to ensure that the detached thread continues execution for the lifetime of the application.

pure / const

The pure attribute specifies that a function has no effects except the return value. That is to say, the return value of a pure function depends only on the parameters and/or global variables. Such a function can undergo the same subexpression elimination and loop optimization as an arithmetic operator.

The const attribute specifies that a function does not examine any values except their arguments, and have no side-effects except the return value. Note that a function with pointer arguments or calls a non-const function usually should not be const. It similarly doesn't make sense for a const function to return void. const can be thought as a stricter form of pure since it doesn't depend on global values or pointers.

```
int square(int n) __attribute__((const));
```

pure and const are both attributes that invoke the functional programming paradigm to allow for significant performance optimizations. For example, because the result of a function declared const does not depend on anything other than the arguments passed in, computed results can be cached and returned the next time that combination of arguments is passed.

unused

This attribute, when attached to a function, denotes that the function is not meant to be used. GCC will not produce a warning for this function.

The same effect can be accomplished with the __unused keyword.

Declare this on parameters that are not used in the method implementation. Knowing that little bit of context allows the compiler to make optimizations accordingly. You're most likely to use __unused in delegate method implementations, since protocols frequently provide more context than is often necessary, in order to satisfy a large number of potential use cases.

LLVM

Like many features of GCC, Clang supports __attribute__, adding its own small set of extensions.

To check the availability of a particular attribute, you can use the __has_attribute directive.

availability

Clang introduces the availability attribute, which can be placed on declarations to availability for particular operating system versions. Consider the function declaration for a hypothetical function f:

```
void f(void) __attribute__((availability(macosx,
introduced=10.4,deprecated=10.6,obsoleted=10.7)));
```

In this case, the attribute states that f was introduced in Mac OS X 10.4, deprecated in Mac OS X 10.6, and obsoleted in Mac OS X 10.7.

This information is used by Clang to determine when it is safe to use f. If Clang is instructed to compile code for Mac OS X 10.5, a call to f() succeeds. If Clang is instructed to compile code for Mac OS X 10.6, the call succeeds but Clang emits a warning specifying that the function is deprecated. Finally, if Clang is instructed to compile code for Mac OS X 10.7, the call fails because f() is no longer available.

The availability attribute takes a comma-separated list or arguments starting with the platform name, followed by clauses specifying important milestones in the declaration's lifetime, and other information. The order of these arguments does not matter.

- introduced: The first version in which this declaration was introduced.

- deprecated: The first version in which this declaration was deprecated, meaning that users should migrate away from this API.

- obsoleted: The first version in which this declaration was obsoleted, meaning that it was removed completely and can no longer be used.

- unavailable: This declaration is never available on this platform.

- message: Additional message text that Clang will provide when emitting a warning or error about use of a deprecated or obsoleted declaration. Useful for directing users to replacement APIs.

Multiple availability attributes can be placed on a declaration, with each used for a particular platform. Only the availability attribute for the target platform will be used; any others will be ignored. If no availability attribute is specified for the current target platform, the availability attributes are ignored.

Supported Platforms

- ios: Apple's iOS operating system. The minimum deployment target is specified by the -mios-version-min=*version* or -miphoneos-version-min=*version* command-line arguments.

- macosx: Apple's Mac OS X operating system. The minimum deployment target is specified by the -mmacosx-version-min=*version* command-line argument.

overloadable

Clang provides support for C++ function overloading in C with the overloadable attribute. For example, one might provide several overloaded versions of a tgsin function that invokes the appropriate standard function computing the sine of a value with float, double, or long double precision:

```
#include <math.h>
float __attribute__((overloadable)) tgsin(float x)
{ return sinf(x); }
double __attribute__((overloadable)) tgsin(double x)
{ return sin(x); }
long double __attribute__((overloadable)) tgsin(long
double x) { return sinl(x); }
```

Overloadable only works for functions. One can overload method declarations to some extent by using generic return and parameter types, like id and void *.

Context is king when it comes to compiler optimizations. By providing constraints on how to interpret code, the generated assembly is likely to be more efficient. Meet the compiler halfway, and you'll always be rewarded.

And __attribute__ isn't just for the compiler either: the next person to see the code will appreciate the extra context, too. So go the extra mile for the benefit of your collaborator, successor, or just 2-years-from-now-(and-you've-forgotten-everything-about–this-code) you.

Because in the end, the love you take is equal to the love you make.

instancetype

Objective-C is evolving rapidly, in a way that you just don't see in established programming languages.

ARC, object literals, subscripting, blocks: in the span of just three years, so much of how we program in Objective-C has been changed (for the better).

All of this innovation is a result of Apple's philosophy of vertical integration. Just as Apple's investment in custom chip design has allowed them to compete aggressively with their mobile hardware, so their investment in LLVM have allowed their software to keep pace.

Clang developments can range from the mundane to paradigm-changing, but telling the difference takes practice. Because we're talking about low-level language features, it's difficult to understand what implications they may have for high-level API design.

One such example is instancetype.

In Objective-C, conventions aren't just a matter of best-practices, they are implicit instructions to the compiler.

For example, alloc and init both have return types of id, yet in Xcode, the compiler makes all of the correct type checks. How is this possible?

In Cocoa, there is a convention that methods with names like alloc, or init always return objects that are an instance of the receiver class. These methods are said to have a related result type.

Class constructor methods, although they similarly return id, don't get the same type-checking benefit, because they don't follow that naming convention.

You can try this out for yourself:

```
[[[NSArray alloc] init] mediaPlaybackAllowsAirPlay];
// ! "No visible @interface for `NSArray` declares the
selector `mediaPlaybackAllowsAirPlay`"

[[NSArray array] mediaPlaybackAllowsAirPlay];
// (No error)
```

Because alloc and init follow the naming convention for related result types, the correct type check against NSArray is performed. However, the equivalent class constructor array does not follow that convention, and is interpreted as a generic id.

id is useful for opting-out of type safety, but that's not the objective here.

The alternative, of explicitly declaring the return type ((NSArray *) in the previous example) fixes the type safety problem, but doesn't play nicely with subclasses.

This is where the compiler steps in to resolve the situation:

instancetype is a contextual keyword that can be used as a result type to signal that a method returns a related result type. For example:

```
@interface Person
+ (instancetype)personWithName:(NSString *)name;
@end
```

With instancetype, the compiler will correctly infer that the result of +personWithName: is an instance of a Person.

---

instancetype, unlike id, can only be used as the result type in a method declaration.

---

instancetype is just one of the many language extensions to Objective-C, with more being added with each new OS & Xcode release. Take it as an example of how paying attention to the low-level details can give you insights into powerful new ways to transform Objective-C.

NS_ENUM & NS_OPTIONS

When everything is an object, nothing is.

That is to say: sometimes it's nice to be able to drop down to the C layer of things.

Yes, C—that non-objective part of our favorite Smalltalk-inspired hybrid language—can be a great asset. It's fast, it's battle-tested, it's the very foundation of modern computing. But more than that, C is the escape hatch for when the Object-Oriented paradigm cracks under its own cognitive weight.

- Static functions are nicer than class methods.
- Enums are nicer than string constants.
- Bitmasks are nicer than arrays of string constants.
- Preprocessor directives are nicer than runtime hacks.

Introduced in Foundation with iOS 6 / Mac OS X 10.8, the NS_ENUM and NS_OPTIONS macros are the new, preferred way to declare enum types.

enum, or enumerated value types, are the C way to define constants for fixed values, like days of the week, or available styles of table view cells. In an enum declaration, constants without explicit values will automatically be assigned values sequentially, starting from 0.

There are several ways to declare enums. What's confusing is that there are subtle functional differences between each approach, and without knowing any better, someone is just as likely to use them interchangeably.

For instance:

```
enum {
    UITableViewCellStyleDefault,
    UITableViewCellStyleValue1,
    UITableViewCellStyleValue2,
    UITableViewCellStyleSubtitle
};
```

...declares integer values, but no type.

Whereas:

```
typedef enum {
    UITableViewCellStyleDefault,
    UITableViewCellStyleValue1,
    UITableViewCellStyleValue2,
    UITableViewCellStyleSubtitle
} UITableViewCellStyle;
```

...defines the UITableViewCellStyle type, suitable for method parameters or function arguments.

Apple had previously defined all of their enum types as:

```
typedef enum {
    UITableViewCellStyleDefault,
    UITableViewCellStyleValue1,
    UITableViewCellStyleValue2,
    UITableViewCellStyleSubtitle
};

    typedef NSInteger UITableViewCellStyle;
```

...which ensures a fixed size for UITableViewCellStyle, but does nothing to hint the relation between the aforementioned enum and the new type to the compiler.

Thankfully, Apple has decided on "One Macro To Rule Them All" with NS_ENUM.

NS_ENUM

Now, UITableViewCellStyle is declared with:

```
typedef NS_ENUM(NSInteger, UITableViewCellStyle) {
    UITableViewCellStyleDefault,
    UITableViewCellStyleValue1,
    UITableViewCellStyleValue2,
    UITableViewCellStyleSubtitle
};
```

The first argument for NS_ENUM is the storage type of the new type. In a 64-bit environment, UITableViewCellStyle will be 8 bytes long—same as NSInteger. If the specified size cannot fit all of the defined values, an error will be generated by the compiler. The second argument is the name of the new type. Inside the code block, the values are defined as usual.

This approach combines the best of all of the aforementioned approaches, and even provides additional hints to the compiler for type-checking.

NS_OPTIONS

enum values can also be used to define a bitmask. Using a convenient property of binary arithmetic, a single integer value can simultaneously encode a combination of values all at once using the bitwise OR (|), and decoded with bitwise AND (&). Each subsequent value, rather than automatically being incremented by 1 from 0, are manually given a value with a bit offset: 1 << 0, 1 << 1, 1 << 2, and so on.

If you imagine the binary representation of a number, like 10110 for 22, each individual bit can be though to represent a single boolean value.

Bitmasks are constructed with the NS_OPTIONS macro.

In UIKit, for example, UIViewAutoresizing is a bitmask that can represent any combination of flexible top, bottom, left, and right margins, or width and height.

```
typedef NS_OPTIONS(NSUInteger, UIViewAutoresizing) {
    UIViewAutoresizingNone              = 0,
    UIViewAutoresizingFlexibleLeftMargin  = 1 << 0,
    UIViewAutoresizingFlexibleWidth       = 1 << 1,
    UIViewAutoresizingFlexibleRightMargin = 1 << 2,
    UIViewAutoresizingFlexibleTopMargin   = 1 << 3,
    UIViewAutoresizingFlexibleHeight      = 1 << 4,
    UIViewAutoresizingFlexibleBottomMargin = 1 << 5
};
```

The syntax is exactly the same as NS_ENUM, but NS_OPTIONS alerts the compiler that values can be combined with bitmask |.

A skilled Objective-C developer is able to gracefully switch between the Objective and Procedural paradigms, and use each to their respective advantage.

NS_ENUM and NS_OPTIONS are handy additions to the Objective-C development experience, and reaffirm the healthy dialectic between its objective and procedural nature. Keep this in mind as you move forward in your own journey to understand the logical tensions that underpin everything around us.

Foundation & CoreFoundation

Key-Value Coding Collection Operators

Rubyists laugh at Objective-C's bloated syntax.

Although we lost a few pounds over the summer with our sleek new object literals, those Red-headed bullies still taunt us with their map one-liners and their fancy Symbol#to_proc.

A lot of how elegant a language is perceived to be comes down to how well it avoids loops. for, while; even for-in fast enumeration expressions are a drag. No matter how they're sugar-coated, loops are a block of code that can be otherwise expressed more simply in natural language:.

"get the average salary of these employees", versus:

```
double totalSalary = 0.0;
for (Employee *employee in employees) {
  totalSalary += [employee.salary doubleValue];
}
double averageSalary = totalSalary / [employees count];
```

Meh.

Fortunately, Key-Value Coding provides a much more concise —almost Ruby-like—way to do this:

```
[employees valueForKeyPath:@"@avg.salary"];
```

KVC Collection Operators allows actions to be performed on a collection using key path notation in valueForKeyPath:. @'s in a key path denote an aggregate function whose result can be returned or chained, just like any other key path.

Collection Operators fall into one of three different categories, according to the kind of value they return:

- Simple Collection Operators return strings, numbers, or dates, depending on the operator.
- Object Operators return an array.
- Array and Set Operators return an array or set, depending on the operator.

The best way to understand how these work is to see them in action. Consider a Product class, and a products array with the following data:

Product.h

```
@interface Product : NSObject
@property NSString *name;
@property double price;
@property NSDate *launchedOn;
@end
```

Name	Price	Launch Date
iPhone 5	$ 199	September 21, 2012
iPad mini	$ 329	November 2, 2012
MacBook Pro	$ 1,699	June 11, 2012
iMac	$ 1,299	November 2, 2012

Simple Collection Operators

- @count: Returns the number of objects in the collection.

- @sum: Converts each object in the collection to a double, computes the sum, and returns the sum.

- @avg: Takes the double value of each object in the collection, and returns the average value.

- @max: Determines the maximum value using compare:. Objects must support mutual comparison for this to work.

- @min: Same as @max, but returns the minimum value.

Example

```
[products valueForKeyPath:@"@count"]; // 4
[products valueForKeyPath:@"@sum.price"]; // 3526.00
[products valueForKeyPath:@"@avg.price"]; // 881.50
[products valueForKeyPath:@"@max.price"]; // 1699.00
[products valueForKeyPath:@"@min.launchedOn"];
// June 11, 2012
```

To get the aggregate value of an array or set of NSNumbers, simply pass self as the key path after the operator,
e.g. [@[@(1), @(2), @(3)] valueForKeyPath:@"@max.self"]

Object Operators

Consider another example, with an array representing the current stock of a local Apple store (which is running low on iPad Mini, and doesn't have the new iMac):

```
NSArray *inventory = @[iPhone5, iPhone5, iPhone5,
iPadMini, macBookPro, macBookPro];
```

- @unionOfObjects / @distinctUnionOfObjects: Returns an array of the objects in the property specified in the key path to the right of the operator. @distinctUnionOfObjects removes duplicates, whereas @unionOfObjects does not.

Example

```
[inventory valueForKeyPath:@"@unionOfObjects.name"];
// "iPhone 5", "iPhone 5", "iPhone 5", "iPad mini",
"MacBook Pro", "MacBook Pro"

[inventory
valueForKeyPath:@"@distinctUnionOfObjects.name"];
// "iPhone 5", "iPad mini", "MacBook Pro"
```

Array and Set Operators

Array and Set Operators are similar to Object Operators, except that they work on collections of NSArray and NSSet.

- @distinctUnionOfArrays / @unionOfArrays: Returns an array containing the combined values of each array in the collection, as specified by the key path to the right of the operator. The distinct version removes duplicate values.

- @distinctUnionOfSets: Similar to @distinctUnionOfArrays, but it expects an NSSet containing NSSet objects, and returns an NSSet. Because sets can't contain duplicate values anyway, there is only the distinct operator.

Example

```
telecomStoreInventory = @[iPhone5, iPhone5, iPadMini];

[@[appleStoreInventory, telecomStoreInventory]
valueForKeyPath:@"@distinctUnionOfArrays.name"];
// "iPhone 5", "MacBook Pro"
```

KVC Collection Operators are a must-know for anyone wanting to save a few extra lines of code and look cool in the process.

While scripting languages like Ruby boast considerably more flexibility in its one-liner capability, perhaps we should take a moment to celebrate the restraint built into Objective-C and Collection Operators.

Key-Value Observing

Ask anyone who's been around the NSBlock a few times: Key-Value Observing has the worst API in all of Cocoa.

It's awkward, verbose, and confusing. And worst of all, its terrible API belies one of the most compelling features of the framework.

When dealing with complicated stateful systems, dutiful book-keeping is essential for maintaining sanity. Lest the right hand not know what the left hand doeth, objects benefit from a way to publish and subscribe to state changes over time.

In Objective-C and Cocoa, there are several ways that events are communicated, each with varying degrees of formality and coupling:

- NSNotification & NSNotificationCenter provide a centralized hub through which any part of an application may notify and be notified of changes from any other part of the application. The only requirement is to know what to listen for, specifically the notification name. For example, UIApplicationDidReceiveMemoryWarningNotification signals a low memory environment in an application.

- Key-Value Observing allows for ad-hoc, evented introspection between specific object instances by listening for changes on a particular key path. For example, a UIProgressView might observe the numberOfBytesRead of a network request to derive and update its own progress property.

- Delegates are a popular pattern for signaling events over a fixed set of methods to a designated handler. For example, UIScrollView sends scrollViewDidScroll: to its delegate each time its scroll offset changes.

- Callbacks of various sorts. For example, block properties like NSOperation -completionBlock, or C function pointers passed as hooks into functions like SCNetworkReachabilitySetCallback(3).

Of all of these methods, Key-Value Observing is arguably the least well-understood. So this week, NSHipster will endeavor to provide some much-needed clarification and notion of best practices to this situation.

<NSKeyValueObserving>, or KVO, is an informal protocol that defines a common mechanism for observing and notifying state changes between objects. Being an informal protocol, classes don't advertise their conformance to it (it's just implicitly assumed for all subclasses of NSObject).

The main value proposition of KVO is rather compelling: any object can subscribe to be notified about state changes in any other object. Most of this is built-in, automatic, and transparent.

Similar manifestations of this observer pattern are the secret sauce of most modern Javascript frameworks, like Backbone.js and Ember.js.

Subscribing

Objects can have observers added for a particular key path, those dot-separated keys that specify a sequence of properties. Most of the time with KVO, these are just the top-level properties on the object.

The method used to add an observer is addObserver:forKeyPath:options:context:

```
- (void)addObserver:(NSObject *)observer
     forKeyPath:(NSString *)keyPath
        options:(NSKeyValueObservingOptions)options
        context:(void *)context
```

- observer: The object to register for KVO notifications. The observer must implement the key-value observing method observeValueForKeyPath:ofObject:change:context:.

- keyPath: The key path, relative to the receiver, of the property to observe. This value must not be nil.

- options: A combination of the NSKeyValueObservingOptions values that specifies what is included in observation notifications. For possible values, see "NSKeyValueObservingOptions".

- context: Arbitrary data that is passed to observer in observeValueForKeyPath:ofObject:change:context:.

Yuck. What makes this API so unsightly is the fact that those last two parameters are almost always 0 and NULL, respectively.

options refers to a bitmask of NSKeyValueObservingOptions.

NSKeyValueObservingOptions

- NSKeyValueObservingOptionNew: Indicates that the change dictionary should provide the new attribute value.

- NSKeyValueObservingOptionOld: Indicates that the change dictionary should contain the old attribute value.

- NSKeyValueObservingOptionInitial: If specified, a notification should be sent to the observer immediately, before the observer registration method even returns. The change dictionary in the notification will always contain an NSKeyValueChangeNewKey entry if NSKeyValueObservingOptionNew is also specified but will never contain an NSKeyValueChangeOldKey entry. (In an initial notification the current value of the observed property may be old, but it's new to the observer.) You can use this option instead of explicitly invoking, at the same time, code that is also invoked by the observer's observeValueForKeyPath:ofObject:change:context: method. When this option is used with addObserver:forKeyPath:options:context: a notification will be sent for each indexed object to which the observer is being added.

- NSKeyValueObservingOptionPrior: Whether separate notifications should be sent to the observer before and after each change, instead of a single notification after the change. The change dictionary in a notification sent before a change always contains an NSKeyValueChangeNotificationIsPriorKey entry whose value is @YES, but never contains an NSKeyValueChangeNewKey entry. When this option is specified the change dictionary in a notification sent after a change contains the same entries that it would contain if this option were not specified. You can use this option when the observer's own key-value observing-compliance requires it to invoke one of the -willChange... methods for one of its own properties, and the value of that property depends on the value of the observed object's property. (In that situation it's too late to easily invoke -willChange... properly in response to receiving an observeValueForKeyPath:ofObject:change:context: message after the change.)

As for context, this parameter is a value that can be used later to differentiate between observations of different objects with the same key path.

Responding

Another ugly aspect of KVO is the fact that there is no way to specify custom selectors to handle observations, as one might be used to from the Target-Action pattern used by controls.

Instead, all changes for observers are funneled through a single method:

```
- (void)observeValueForKeyPath:(NSString *)keyPath
                      ofObject:(id)object
                        change:(NSDictionary *)change
                       context:(void *)context
```

Those parameters are the same as what were specified in – addObserver:forKeyPath:options:context:, save for change, which is populated from the NSKeyValueObservingOptions options passed when the observer was originally added.

Here's a typical implementation of this method:

```
- (void)observeValueForKeyPath:(NSString *)keyPath
                      ofObject:(id)object
                        change:(NSDictionary *)change
                       context:(void *)context
{
    if ([keyPath isEqualToString:@"state"]) {
        // ...
    }
}
```

Depending on how many kinds of objects are being observed by a single class, this method may also introduce isKindOfObject: or respondsToSelector: in order to definitively identify the kind of event being passed.

However, the safest method is to do an equality check to context—especially when dealing with subclasses whose parents observe the same keypath.

Correct Context Declarations

What makes a good context value? Here's a suggestion:

```
static void * XXContext = &XXContext;
```

It's that simple: a static value that stores its own pointer. It means nothing on its own, which makes it rather perfect for <NSKeyValueObserving>:

```
- (void)observeValueForKeyPath:(NSString *)keyPath
                      ofObject:(id)object
                        change:(NSDictionary *)change
                       context:(void *)context
{
  if (context == XXContext) {
    if ([keyPath isEqualToString:@"isFinished")])]) {
      //...
    }
  }
}
```

Better Key Paths

Passing strings as key paths is strictly worse than using properties directly, as any typo or misspelling will break things, and can't be caught by the compiler.

A clever workaround to this is to use NSStringFromSelector with a @selector literal value:

```
NSStringFromSelector(@selector(isFinished))
```

Since @selector looks through all available selectors in the target, this won't prevent all mistakes, but it will catch most of them—including breaking changes made by Xcode automatic refactoring tool.

```
- (void)observeValueForKeyPath:(NSString *)keyPath
                      ofObject:(id)object
                        change:(NSDictionary *)change
                       context:(void *)context
{
    if (context == XXContext) {
        if ([keyPath isEqualToString:
NSStringFromSelector(@selector(isFinished))]) {
            // ...
        }
    }
}
```

Unsubscribing

When an observer is done listening for changes on an object, it is expected to call removeObserver:forKeyPath:context:. This will often either be called in dealloc, or a similar finalization method.

Safe Unsubscribe with @try / @catch

Perhaps the most profound annoyance about KVO is that if an object calls removeObserver:forKeyPath:context: when the object is not registered as an observer (whether it was already unregistered or not registered in the first place), an exception is thrown. The kicker is that there's not built-in way to even check if an object is registered!

Which causes one to rely on a rather unfortunate cudgel @try with an unhandled @catch:

```
- (void)observeValueForKeyPath:(NSString *)keyPath
                      ofObject:(id)object
                        change:(NSDictionary *)change
                       context:(void *)context
{
    if ([keyPath
isEqualToString:NSStringFromSelector(@selector(isFinishe
d))]) {
        if ([object isFinished]) {
            @try {
                [object removeObserver:self
forKeyPath:NSStringFromSelector(@selector(isFinished))];
            }
            @catch (NSException * __unused exception) {}
        }
    }
}
```

Granted, not handling a caught exception, as in this example, is waving the [UIColor whiteColor] flag of surrender. One should only really use this technique when faced with intermittent crashes which cannot be remedied by normal book-keeping (whether due to race conditions or undocumented behavior from a superclass).

Automatic Property Notifications

KVO is made useful by its near-universal adoption. Much of the setup is automatically taken care of by the compiler and runtime.

Classes can opt-out of automatic KVO by overriding +automaticallyNotifiesObserversForKey: and returning NO.

But what about compound or derived values? For example, consider an object with a @dynamic, readonly address property, which reads and formats its streetAddress, locality, region, and postalCode?

One could implement keyPathsForValuesAffectingAddress (or the generic +keyPathsForValuesAffectingValueForKey:):

```
+ (NSSet *)keyPathsForValuesAffectingAddress {
    return [NSSet setWithObjects:
NSStringFromSelector(@selector(streetAddress)),
NSStringFromSelector(@selector(locality)),
NSStringFromSelector(@selector(region)),
NSStringFromSelector(@selector(postalCode)), nil];
}
```

So there you have it: some general observations and best practices for KVO. To an enterprising NSHipster, KVO can be a powerful substrate on top of which clever and powerful abstractions can be built.

Use it wisely, and understand the rules and conventions to make the most of it in your own application.

NSError

To err is human.
To NSError is Cocoa.

All programs on a Unix system are a child process of another process, forking all the way from the original process: pid 1 (which in the case of Mac OS X is launchd).

When an executable finishes, it communicates a status code between 0 and 255 to its parent, as a way to communicate why or how the process exited. 0 means "everything exited normally; nothing to report here", while any non-zero value indicates something that the parent process should be aware of. Exit status codes may be used to indicate whether the process crashed or terminated prematurely. By some conventions, the higher the return value, the more dire the circumstances.

In an OO paradigm, processes are abstracted away, leaving only objects and the messages they pass between one another. That distinction between success and failure (and between different varieties of failure) is still useful in object-oriented programming. But considering that methods are often wont to return values other than BOOL to indicate success or failure, this can create something of a predicament.

Languages more drama-prone and trigger-happy than Objective-C reconcile this by abusing the hell out of exceptions, raising at even the slightest breach in contract. To our good fortune as Cocoanauts, however, Objective-C takes a more civilized approach when it comes to giving us bad news, and that approach is NSError.

NSError is the unsung hero of the Foundation framework. Passed gallantly in and out of perilous method calls, it is the messenger by which we are able to contextualize our failures.

NSError is toll-free bridged with CFError, but it's unlikely to find a reason to dip down to its Core Foundation counterpart.

Each NSError object encodes three critical pieces of information: a status code, corresponding to a particular error domain, as well as additional context provided by a userInfo dictionary.

code & domain

Like exit status codes, an NSError -code signals the nature of the problem. These status codes are defined within a particular error domain, in order to avoid overlap and confusion. These status codes are generally defined by constants in an enum.

For example, in the NSCocoaErrorDomain, the status code for an error caused by NSFileManager attempting to access a non-existent file is 4 (NSFileNoSuchFileError). However, 4 in NSPOSIXErrorDomain refers to a POSIX EINTR, or "interrupted function" error.

Now, anyone coming from a systems programming background may have just had a vision of a switch statement with smatterings of printf, to translate numeric constants into something human-readable. NSError is way ahead of you.

userInfo

What gives NSError its particular charm is everyone's favorite grab bag property: userInfo. As a convention throughout Cocoa, userInfo is a dictionary that contains arbitrary key-value pairs that, whether for reasons of subclassing or schematic sparsity, are not suited to full-fledged properties.

In the case of NSError, there are several special keys that correspond to readonly properties.

Three are generally useful:

- localizedDescription (NSLocalizedDescriptionKey): A localized description of the error.

- localizedRecoverySuggestion (NSLocalizedRecoverySuggestionErrorKey): A localized recovery suggestion for the error.

- localizedFailureReason (NSLocalizedFailureReasonErrorKey): A localized explanation of the reason for the error.

...whereas three others are specific to OS X:

- localizedRecoveryOptions (NSLocalizedRecoveryOptionsErrorKey): An array containing the localized titles of buttons appropriate for displaying in an alert panel

- recoveryAttempter (NSRecoveryAttempterErrorKey)

- helpAnchor (NSHelpAnchorErrorKey): Used by an alert panel by a help anchor button.

Here's how to construct NSError with a userInfo dictionary:

```objc
NSDictionary *userInfo = @{
  NSLocalizedDescriptionKey: NSLocalizedString(
@"Operation was unsuccessful.", nil),

  NSLocalizedFailureReasonErrorKey: NSLocalizedString(
@"The operation timed out.", nil),

  NSLocalizedRecoverySuggestionErrorKey:
NSLocalizedString(@"Have you tried turning it off and on
again?", nil)
                        };

NSError *error =
    [NSError errorWithDomain:NSHipsterErrorDomain
                        code:-57
                    userInfo:userInfo];
```

The advantage of encapsulating this information in an object like NSError, as opposed to, say, throwing exceptions willy-nilly, is that these error objects can be passed between different objects and contexts.

For example, a controller that calls a method with an out NSError ** parameter might pass that error into an alert view on failure:

```
[[[UIAlertView alloc]
    initWithTitle:error.localizedDescription
        message:error.localizedRecoverySuggestion
        delegate:nil
cancelButtonTitle:NSLocalizedString(@"OK", nil)
otherButtonTitles:nil, nil] show];
```

One clever hack used by C functions to communicate errors is to encode 4-letter ASCII sequences in the 32 bit return type. It's no localizedDescription, but it's better than cross-referencing error codes from a table every time!

For sake of completeness: here is a list of the standard NSError userInfo keys:

- NSLocalizedDescriptionKey
- NSLocalizedFailureReasonErrorKey
- NSLocalizedRecoverySuggestionErrorKey
- NSLocalizedRecoveryOptionsErrorKey
- NSFilePathErrorKey
- NSStringEncodingErrorKey
- NSUnderlyingErrorKey
- NSRecoveryAttempterErrorKey
- NSHelpAnchorErrorKey

Using NSError

There are two ways in which you will encounter NSError: as a consumer and as a producer.

Consuming

As a consumer, you are primarily concerned with methods that have a final parameter of type NSError **. Again, this is to get around the single return value constraint of Objective-C; by passing a pointer to an uninitialized NSError *, that variable will be populated with any error the method populates:

```
NSError *error = nil;
BOOL success = [[NSFileManager defaultManager]
    moveItemAtPath:@"/path/to/target"
            toPath:@"/path/to/destination"
             error:&error];
if (!success) {
    NSLog(@"%@", error);
}
```

---

*According to Cocoa conventions, methods returning BOOL to indicate success or failure are encouraged to have a final NSError ** parameter if there are multiple failure conditions to distinguish.*

A good guideline is whether you could imagine that NSError bubbling up, and being presented to the user.

Another way NSError objects are passed is by way of completionHandler block arguments. This gets around both a constraint on single value returns, as well as values being returned synchronously. This has become especially popular with newer Foundation APIs, like NSURLSession:

```objc
NSURL *URL =
    [NSURL URLWithString:@"http://example.com"];

NSURLRequest *request =
    [NSURLRequest requestWithURL:URL];

NSURLSession *session =
    [NSURLSession sessionWithConfiguration:
        [NSURLSessionConfiguration
            defaultSessionConfiguration]];

[[session dataTaskWithRequest:request
        completionHandler:
^(NSData *data, NSURLResponse *response, NSError *error)
{
    if (error) {
        NSLog(@"%@", error);
    } else {
        // ...
    }
}] resume];
```

Producing

One would be well-advised to follow the same conventions for error handling as other Foundation classes. In situations where a custom method invokes a method with an NSError ** parameter, it is usually a good idea to similarly pass that NSError ** parameter into the signature of the custom method. More substantial apps or libraries are encouraged to define their own error domains and error code constants as suitable.

To pass an error to an NSError ** parameter, do the following:

```
- (BOOL)validateObject:(id)object
                error:(NSError *__autoreleasing *)error
{
    BOOL success = // ...

    if (!success & error) {
      *error = [NSError
                errorWithDomain:NSHipsterErrorDomain
                           code:-42
                       userInfo:nil];
      return NO;
    }

    return YES;
}
```

NSOperation

Everyone knows that the secret to making an app snappy and responsive is to offload computation to the background. The modern Objective-C developer, thus has two options: Grand Central Dispatch & NSOperation.

Since GCD has gone pretty mainstream, let's focus on the latter, object-oriented approach.

NSOperation represents a single unit of computation. It's an abstract class that gives subclasses a useful, thread-safe way to model aspects like state, priority, dependencies, and cancellation.

If subclassing isn't your cup of tea, there's always NSBlockOperation, a concrete subclass that wraps block in operations.

Examples of tasks that lend themselves well to NSOperation include network requests, image resizing, linguistic processing, or any other repeatable, structured, long-running task that produces useful data.

But simply wrapping computation into an object doesn't do much without a little oversight. That's where NSOperationQueue comes in.

NSOperationQueue regulates the concurrent execution of operations. It acts as a priority queue, such that operations are executed in a roughly First-In-First-Out manner, with higher-priority ones getting to jump ahead of lower-priority ones. NSOperationQueue can also executes operations concurrently, with the option to limit the maximum number to be executed simultaneously, with the maxConcurrentOperationCount property.

To kick off an NSOperation, one can either call -start, or add it to an NSOperationQueue, which will automatically start the operation when it reaches the front of the queue.

State

NSOperation encodes a simple state machine to describe the execution of an operation:

isReady → isExecuting → isFinished

In lieu of an explicit state property, state is determined implicitly by KVO notifications on those keypaths. That is, when an operation is ready to be executed, it sends a KVO notification for the isReady keypath, whose corresponding property would then return YES.

Each property must be mutually exclusive from one-another in order to encode a consistent state:

- isReady: Returns YES to indicate that the operation is ready to execute, or NO if there are still unfinished initialization steps on which it is dependent.

- isExecuting: Returns YES if the operation is currently executing, or NO otherwise.

- isFinished: Returns YES if the operation finished execution successfully, or if the operation was cancelled. An NSOperationQueue does not dequeue an operation until isFinished changes to YES, so it is critical to implement this correctly in order to avoid deadlocks.

Cancellation

It may be useful to cancel operations early to prevent needless work from being performed. Reasons for cancellation may include explicit user action, or a failure in a dependent operation.

Similar to execution state, NSOperation communicates cancellation state through KVO on the isCancelled keypath. When an operation responds to the -cancel command, it should clean up any internal details and arrive in an appropriate final state as quickly as possible. Specifically, the values for both isCancelled and isFinished need to become YES, and the value of isExecuting to NO.

One thing to watch out for are the spelling peculiarities around the word "cancel". Although spelling varies across dialects, when it comes to NSOperation:

- cancel: use one L for the method (verb)
- isCancelled: use two L's for the property (adjective)

Priority

All operations may not be equally important. Setting the queuePriority property will promote or defer an operation in an NSOperationQueue according to the following ranking:

- NSOperationQueuePriorityVeryHigh
- NSOperationQueuePriorityHigh
- NSOperationQueuePriorityNormal
- NSOperationQueuePriorityLow
- NSOperationQueuePriorityVeryLow

Additionally, operations may specify a threadPriority value between 0.0 and 1.0, with 1.0 representing the highest priority. Whereas queuePriority determine the order in which operations are started, threadPriority specifies the allocation of computation once an operation has been started.

But as with most threading details, if you don't know what it does, you probably didn't need to know about it anyway.

Dependencies

Depending on the complexity of your application, it may make sense to divide up large tasks into a series of composable sub-tasks. You can do this using NSOperation dependencies.

For example, to describe the process of of downloading and resizing an image from a server, you would probably want to divide up networking into one operation, and resizing into another. Since, an image can't be resized until its downloaded. Thus, the the networking operation is said to be a dependency of the resizing operation, and must be finished before the resizing operation can be started. Expressed in code:

```
[resizingOperation addDependency:networkingOperation];
[operationQueue addOperation:networkingOperation];
[operationQueue addOperation:resizingOperation];
```

An operation will not be started until all of its dependencies return YES to isFinished. Aperations involved in a dependency graph should be added to the operation queue, lest there be a gap somewhere along the way.

Also, make sure not to create a dependency cycle, such that A depends on B, and B depends on A, for example. This will create deadlock and sadness.

---

completionBlock

One useful feature that was added as part of the blocks renaissance of iOS 4 / Mac OS X 10.6 is the completionBlock property.

When an NSOperation finishes, it will execute its completionBlock exactly once. This provides a convenient way to customize the behavior of an operation when used in a model or view controller. For example, you could set a completion block on a network operation to do something with the response data from the server once its finished loading.

NSOperation remains an essential tool in the modern Objective-C programmers bag of tricks. Whereas GCD is ideal for in-line asynchronous processing, NSOperation provides a more comprehensive, object-oriented model of computation, which is ideal for encapsulating all of the data around structured, repeatable tasks in an application.

Add NSOperation to your next project and bring delight not only to your users, but yourself as well.

NSSortDescriptor

Sorting: it's a mainstay of Computer Science 101 exams and whiteboarding interview questions. But when was the last time you actually needed to know how to implement Quicksort yourself, anyway?

When making apps with high-level frameworks like Cocoa, sorting is just something you can assume to be fast. As such, it becomes a matter of convenience and clarity of intention, and as far as those go, you'd be hard-pressed to find a better implementation than Foundation's NSSortDescriptor.

NSSortDescriptor objects are constructed with the following parameters:

- key: for a given collection, the key for the corresponding value to be sorted on for each object in the collection.

- ascending: a boolean specifying whether the collection should be sorted in ascending (YES) or descending (NO) order.

There is an optional third parameter that relates to how sortable values are compared to one another. By default, this is a simple equality check, but this behavior can be changed by passing either a selector (SEL) or comparator (NSComparator).

Any time you're sorting user-facing strings, be sure to pass the localizedStandardCompare: selector, which will sort according to the language rules of the current locale (locales may differ on ordering of case, diacritics, and so forth).

Collection classes like NSArray and NSSet have methods to return sorted arrays given an array of sortDescriptors. Sort descriptors are applied in order, so that if two elements happen to be tied for a particular sorting criteria, the tie is broken by any subsequent descriptors.

To put that into more concrete terms, consider a Person class with properties for firstName & lastName of type NSString *, and age, which is an NSUInteger.

Person.h

```
@interface Person : NSObject
@property NSString *firstName;
@property NSString *lastName;
@property NSNumber *age;
@end
```

Person.m

```objc
@implementation Person

- (NSString *)description {
    return [NSString stringWithFormat:@"%@ %@",
self.firstName, self.lastName];
}

@end
```

Given the following dataset:

index	0	1	2	3
firstName	Alice	Bob	Charlie	Quentin
lastName	Smith	Jones	Smith	Alberts
age	24	27	33	31

Here are some of the different ways they can be sorted by combinations of NSSortDescriptor:

```objc
NSArray *firstNames =
    @[ @"Alice", @"Bob", @"Charlie", @"Quentin" ];

NSArray *lastNames =
    @[ @"Smith", @"Jones", @"Smith", @"Alberts" ];

NSArray *ages = @[ @24, @27, @33, @31 ];
```

```objc
NSMutableArray *people = [NSMutableArray array];
[firstNames enumerateObjectsUsingBlock:
^(id obj, NSUInteger idx, BOOL *stop)
{
    Person *person = [[Person alloc] init];
    person.firstName = [firstNames objectAtIndex:idx];
    person.lastName = [lastNames objectAtIndex:idx];
    person.age = [ages objectAtIndex:idx];
    [people addObject:person];
}];


NSSortDescriptor *firstNameSortDescriptor =
[NSSortDescriptor sortDescriptorWithKey:@"firstName"
  ascending:YES
  selector:@selector(localizedStandardCompare:)];
NSSortDescriptor *lastNameSortDescriptor =
[NSSortDescriptor sortDescriptorWithKey:@"lastName"
  ascending:YES
  selector:@selector(localizedStandardCompare:)];
NSSortDescriptor *ageSortDescriptor = [NSSortDescriptor
sortDescriptorWithKey:@"age"
  ascending:NO];


NSLog(@"By age: %@", [people
sortedArrayUsingDescriptors:@[ageSortDescriptor]]);
/* "Charlie Smith", "Quentin Alberts",
    "Bob Jones", "Alice Smith" */


NSLog(@"By first name: %@",
  [people sortedArrayUsingDescriptors:
      @[firstNameSortDescriptor]]);
/* "Alice Smith", "Bob Jones",
    "Charlie Smith", "Quentin Alberts" */
```

```
NSLog(@"By last name, first name: %@",
 [people sortedArrayUsingDescriptors:
      @[lastNameSortDescriptor,
         firstNameSortDescriptor]]);
/* "Quentin Alberts", "Bob Jones",
    "Alice Smith", "Charlie Smith" */
```

NSSortDescriptor can be found throughout Foundation and other system frameworks. Anytime your own classes need to define sort ordering, follow the convention of specifying a sortDescriptors parameter.

Because, in reality, sorting should be thought of in terms of business logic, not mathematical formulas and map-reduce functions. In this respect, NSSortDescriptor is a slam dunk, and will have you pining for it anytime you venture out of Objective-C and Cocoa.

NSPredicate

NSPredicate is a Foundation class that specifies how data should be fetched or filtered. Its query language, something between a SQL WHERE clause and a regular expression, provides an expressive, natural language interface to define logical conditions on which a collection is evaluated.

It's easier to show NSPredicate in use, rather than talk about it in the abstract, so we're going to revisit the example data set used in the NSSortDescriptor chapter:

index	0	1	2	3
firstName	Alice	Bob	Charlie	Quentin
lastName	Smith	Jones	Smith	Alberts
age	24	27	33	31

```
NSArray *firstNames =
    @[ @"Alice", @"Bob", @"Charlie", @"Quentin" ];
NSArray *lastNames =
    @[ @"Smith", @"Jones", @"Smith", @"Alberts" ];
NSArray *ages = @[ @24, @27, @33, @31 ];
```

```objc
NSMutableArray *people = [NSMutableArray array];
[firstNames enumerateObjectsUsingBlock:^(id obj,
NSUInteger idx, BOOL *stop) {
    Person *person = [[Person alloc] init];
    person.firstName = firstNames[idx];
    person.lastName = lastNames[idx];
    person.age = ages[idx];
    [people addObject:person];
}];


NSPredicate *bobPredicate = [NSPredicate
  predicateWithFormat:@"firstName = 'Bob'"];
NSPredicate *smithPredicate = [NSPredicate
  predicateWithFormat:@"lastName = %@", @"Smith"];
NSPredicate *thirtiesPredicate = [NSPredicate
  predicateWithFormat:@"age >= 30"];


NSLog(@"Bobs: %@",
[people filteredArrayUsingPredicate:bobPredicate]);
// ["Bob Jones"]


NSLog(@"Smiths: %@",
[people filteredArrayUsingPredicate:smithPredicate]);
// ["Alice Smith", "Charlie Smith"]


NSLog(@"30's: %@",
[people filteredArrayUsingPredicate:thirtiesPredicate]);
// ["Charlie Smith", "Quentin Alberts"]
```

Using NSPredicate with Collections

Foundation provides methods to filter arrays, sets, and dictionaries with predicates.

NSArray & NSSet, have the methods filteredArrayUsingPredicate: and filteredSetUsingPredicate: which return an immutable collection by evaluating a predicate on the receiver. Their mutable counterparts have the method filterUsingPredicate:, which removes any objects that evaluate to NO when running the predicate on the receiver.

NSDictionary can use predicates by filtering its keys or values, which are both NSArray objects.

NSOrderedSet can either create new ordered sets from a filtered NSArray or NSSet, or alternatively, NSMutableOrderedSet can simply removeObjectsInArray:, passing objects filtered with the negated predicate.

Using NSPredicate with Core Data

NSFetchRequest has a predicate property, which specifies the conditions by which managed objects should be retrieved.

The same rules apply as before, except that predicates are evaluated by the persistent store coordinator within a managed object context, rather than collections being filtered in-memory.

Predicate Syntax

Substitutions

- %@ is a var arg substitution for an object value—often a string, number, or date.

- %K is a var arg substitution for a key path.

```
NSPredicate *ageIs33Predicate = [NSPredicate
    predicateWithFormat:@"%K = %@", @"age", @33];

NSLog(@"Age 33: %@",
[people filteredArrayUsingPredicate:ageIs33Predicate]);
// ["Charlie Smith"]
```

- $VARIABLE_NAME is a value that can be substituted with NSPredicate -predicateWithSubstitutionVariables:.

```
NSPredicate *namesBeginningWithLetterPredicate =
[NSPredicate predicateWithFormat:@"(firstName
BEGINSWITH[cd] $letter) OR (lastName BEGINSWITH[cd]
$letter)"];

NSLog(@"'A' Names: %@",
   [people filteredArrayUsingPredicate:
     [namesBeginningWithLetterPredicate
       predicateWithSubstitutionVariables:
         @{@"letter": @"A"}
]]);
// ["Alice Smith", "Quentin Alberts"]
```

Basic Comparisons

- =, ==: The left-hand expression is equal to the right-hand expression.

- >=, =>: The left-hand expression is greater than or equal to the right-hand expression.

- <=, =<: The left-hand expression is less than or equal to the right-hand expression.

- >: The left-hand expression is greater than the right-hand expression.

- <: The left-hand expression is less than the right-hand expression.

- !=, <>: The left-hand expression is not equal to the right-hand expression.

- BETWEEN: The left-hand expression is between, or equal to either of, the values specified in the right-hand side. The right-hand side is a two value array (an array is required to specify order) giving upper and lower bounds. For example, 1 BETWEEN { 0 , 33 }, or $INPUT BETWEEN { $LOWER, $UPPER }.

Basic Compound Predicates

- AND, &&: Logical AND.
- OR, ||: Logical OR.
- NOT, !: Logical NOT.

String Comparisons

String comparisons are case and diacritic sensitive, by default. One can modify an operator using the key characters c and d within square braces to specify case and diacritic insensitivity respectively. For example, firstName BEGINSWITH[cd] $FIRST_NAME.

- BEGINSWITH: The left-hand expression begins with the right-hand expression.

- CONTAINS: The left-hand expression contains the right-hand expression.

- ENDSWITH: The left-hand expression ends with the right-hand expression.

- LIKE: The left hand expression equals the right-hand expression: ? and * are allowed as wildcard characters, where ? matches 1 character and * matches 0 or more characters.

- MATCHES: The left hand expression equals the right hand expression using a regex-style comparison according to ICU v3 (for more details see the ICU User Guide for Regular Expressions).

Aggregate Operations

Relational Operations

- ANY, SOME: Specifies any of the elements in the following expression. For example, ANY children.age < 18.

- ALL: Specifies all of the elements in the following expression. For example, ALL children.age < 18.

- NONE: Specifies none of the elements in the following expression. For example, NONE children.age < 18. This is logically equivalent to NOT (ANY ...).

- IN: Equivalent to an SQL IN operation, the left-hand side must appear in the collection specified by the right-hand side. For example, name IN { 'Ben', 'Melissa', 'Nick' }.

Array Operations

- array[index]: Specifies the element at the specified index in array.

- array[FIRST]: Specifies the first element in array.

- array[LAST]: Specifies the last element in array.

- array[SIZE]: Specifies the size of array.

- Boolean Value Predicates

- TRUEPREDICATE: A predicate that always evaluates to TRUE.

- FALSEPREDICATE: A predicate that always evaluates to FALSE.

NSCompoundPredicate

AND & OR can be used in predicate format strings to create compound predicates. However, the same can be accomplished using an NSCompoundPredicate.

For example, the following predicates are equivalent:

```
[NSCompoundPredicate
  andPredicateWithSubpredicates:@[
    [NSPredicate predicateWithFormat:@"age > 25"],
    [NSPredicate predicateWithFormat:
        @"firstName = %@", @"Quentin"]
  ]
];

[NSPredicate predicateWithFormat:@"(age > 25) AND
  (firstName = %@)", @"Quentin"];
```

While the syntax string literal is certainly easier to type, there are occasions where you may need to combine existing predicates. In these cases, NSCompoundPredicate - andPredicateWithSubpredicates: & - orPredicateWithSubpredicates: is the way to go.

NSComparisonPredicate

Like NSCompoundPredicate, NSComparisonPredicate constructs an NSPredicate from subcomponents—in this case, NSExpressions on the left and right hand sides. Analyzing its class constructor provides a glimpse into the way NSPredicate format strings are parsed:

```
+ (NSPredicate *)predicateWithLeftExpression:
(NSExpression *)lhs
rightExpression:(NSExpression *)rhs
        modifier:(NSComparisonPredicateModifier)modifier
            type:(NSPredicateOperatorType)type
         options:(NSUInteger)options
```

Parameters

- lhs: The left hand expression.

- rhs: The right hand expression.

- modifier: The modifier to apply. (ANY or ALL)

- type: The predicate operator type.

- options: The options to apply. For no options, pass 0.

NSComparisonPredicate Types

```
enum {
    NSLessThanPredicateOperatorType = 0,
    NSLessThanOrEqualToPredicateOperatorType,
    NSGreaterThanPredicateOperatorType,
    NSGreaterThanOrEqualToPredicateOperatorType,
    NSEqualToPredicateOperatorType,
    NSNotEqualToPredicateOperatorType,
    NSMatchesPredicateOperatorType,
    NSLikePredicateOperatorType,
    NSBeginsWithPredicateOperatorType,
    NSEndsWithPredicateOperatorType,
    NSInPredicateOperatorType,
    NSCustomSelectorPredicateOperatorType,
    NSContainsPredicateOperatorType,
    NSBetweenPredicateOperatorType
};
typedef NSUInteger NSPredicateOperatorType;
NSComparisonPredicate Options
```

- NSCaseInsensitivePredicateOption: A case-insensitive predicate. You represent this option in a predicate format string using a [c] following a string operation (for example, "NeXT" like[c] "next").

- NSDiacriticInsensitivePredicateOption: A diacritic-insensitive predicate. You represent this option in a predicate format string using a [d] following a string operation (for example, "naïve" like[d] "naive").

- NSNormalizedPredicateOption: Indicates that the strings to be compared have been preprocessed. This option supersedes NSCaseInsensitivePredicateOption and NSDiacriticInsensitivePredicateOption, and is intended as a performance optimization option. You represent this option in a predicate format string using a [n] following a string operation (for example, "WXYZlan" matches[n] ".lan").

- NSLocaleSensitivePredicateOption: Indicates that strings to be compared using <, <=, =, =>, > should be handled in a locale-aware fashion. You represent this option in a predicate format string using a [l] following one of the <, <=, =, =>, > operators (for example, "straße" >[l] "strasse").

Block Predicates

Can't be bothered to learn the NSPredicate format syntax? Go through the motions with +predicateWithBlock:

```
NSPredicate *shortNamePredicate = [NSPredicate
predicateWithBlock:
^BOOL(id evaluatedObject, NSDictionary *bindings)
{
    return [[evaluatedObject firstName] length] <= 5;
}];

NSLog(@"Short Names: %@", [people
    filteredArrayUsingPredicate:shortNamePredicate]);
// ["Alice Smith", "Bob Jones"]
```

Since blocks can encapsulate any kind of calculation, there is a whole class of queries that can't be expressed with the NSPredicate format string (such as evaluating against values dynamically calculated at run-time). And while its possible to accomplish the same using an NSExpression with a custom selector, blocks provide a convenient interface to get the job done.

NSPredicates created with predicateWithBlock: cannot be used for Core Data fetch requests backed by a SQLite store.

NSPredicate is truly one of the jewels of Cocoa. Other languages would be lucky to have something with half of its capabilities in a third-party framework—let alone the standard library. Having it as a standard-issue component affords us as application and framework developers an incredible amount of leverage in working with data.

NSExpression

Cocoa is the envy of other standard libraries when it comes to querying and arranging information. With NSPredicate, NSSortDescriptor, and an occasional NSFetchRequest, even the most complex data tasks can be reduced into just a few, extremely-understandable lines of code.

If we take a closer look at NSPredicate, we see that it's actually made up of smaller, atomic parts: two NSExpressions (a left-hand value & a right-hand value), compared with an operator (e.g. <, IN, LIKE, etc.).

Because most developers only use NSPredicate by means of +predicateWithFormat:, NSExpression is a relatively obscure class... which is a shame, because NSExpression is quite an incredible piece of functionality in its own right.

Evaluating Math

The first thing one should know about NSExpression is that it lives to reduce terms. If you think about the process of evaluating an NSPredicate, there are two terms and a comparator. Those two terms need to simplify into something that the operator can handle—very much like the process of compiling a line of code.

Which leads us to NSExpression's first trick: doing math.

```
NSExpression *expression =
    [NSExpression expressionWithFormat:@"4 + 5 - 2**3"];
id value =
    [expression expressionValueWithObject:nil
                                  context:nil];
// 1
```

Boom. Calculator.app in a single line of code.

Functions

But this is only scratching the surface with NSExpression.

Not impressed by a computer doing primary-school maths? How about high school statistics, then?

```
NSArray *numbers = @[@1, @2, @3, @4, @4, @5, @9, @11];
NSExpression *expression =
  [NSExpression expressionForFunction:@"stddev:"
                          arguments:@[[NSExpression
           expressionForConstantValue:numbers]]];

id value =
  [expression expressionValueWithObject:nil
                            context:nil];
// 3.21859...
```

NSExpression functions take a given number of sub-expression arguments. For instance, in the example above, in order to get the standard deviation of the collection, the array of numbers had to be wrapped with +expressionForConstantValue:. It's a minor inconvenience, enough to trip up anyone trying things out for the first time.

Found the Key-Value Coding Simple Collection Operators (@avg, @sum, et al.) lacking? NSExpression's statistical, arithmetic, and bitwise functions are sure to impress.

According to Apple's documentation for NSExpression, there is apparently no overlap between the availability of functions between Mac OS X & iOS. It would appear that recent versions of iOS do, indeed, support functions like stddev:, but this is not reflected in headers or documentation.

Statistics

- average:
- sum:
- count:
- min:
- max:
- median:
- mode:
- stddev:

Basic Arithmetic

These functions take two NSExpression objects representing numbers.

- add:to:
- from:subtract:
- multiply:by:
- divide:by:
- modulus:by:
- abs:

Advanced Arithmetic

- sqrt:
- log:
- ln:
- raise:toPower:
- exp:

Bounding Functions

- ceiling: - the smallest integral value not less than the value in the array
- trunc: - the integral value nearest to but no greater than the value in the array

Functions Shadowing math.h Functions

So mentioned, because ceiling is easily confused with ceil(3). Whereas ceiling acts on an array of numbers, while ceil(3) takes a double (and doesn't have a corresponding built-in NSExpression function). floor: acts the same as floor(3).

- floor:

Random Functions

Two variations—one with and one without an argument. Taking no argument, random returns an equivalent of rand(3), while random: takes a random element from the NSExpression of an array of numbers.

- random
- random:

Binary Arithmetic

- bitwiseAnd:with:
- bitwiseOr:with:
- bitwiseXor:with:
- leftshift:by:
- rightshift:by:
- onesComplement:

Date Functions

- now

String Functions

- lowercase:
- uppercase:

Custom Functions

In addition to the built-in functions, it's possible to invoke custom functions in an NSExpression.

First, define the corresponding method in a category:

```
@interface NSNumber (Factorial)
- (NSNumber *)factorial;
@end

@implementation NSNumber (Factorial)
- (NSNumber *)factorial {
    return @(tgamma([self doubleValue] + 1));
}
@end
```

Then, use the function thusly:

```
NSExpression *expression = [NSExpression
expressionWithFormat:@"FUNCTION(4.2, 'factorial')"];
id value = [expression expressionValueWithObject:nil
context:nil]; // 32.578...
```

The FUNCTION() macro in +expressionWithFormat: is shorthand for the process of building out with -expressionForFunction:

The advantage here, over calling -factorial directly is the ability to invoke the function in an NSPredicate query.

For example, a location:withinRadius: method might be defined to easily query managed objects that are nearby a user's current location.

The use cases are rather marginal, but it's certainly an interesting trick to have in your repertoire.

Together with NSPredicate, NSExpression reminds us what a treat Foundation is: a framework that is not only incredibly useful, but meticulously architected and engineered, to be taken as inspiration for how we should write our own code.

NSFileManager

File systems are a complex topic, with decades of history, vestigial complexities, and idiosyncrasies, and is well outside the scope of this book. And since most applications don't often interact with the file system much beyond simple file operations, one can get away with only knowing the basics.

NSFileManager is Foundation's high-level API for working with file systems. It abstracts Unix and Finder internals, providing a convenient way to create, read, move, copy, and delete files & directories on local or networked drives, as well as iCloud ubiquitous containers.

What follows are some code samples for your copy-pasting pleasure. Use them as a starting point for understanding how to adjust parameters to your particular use case:

Common Tasks

Throughout these code samples is a magical incantation:

NSSearchPathForDirectoriesInDomains(NSDocumentDirectory, NSUserDomainMask, YES).

This may be tied with KVO as one of the worst APIs in Cocoa. Just know that it returns an array containing the user documents directory at index 0. Thank goodness for NSArray -firstObject.

Determining If A File Exists

```
NSFileManager *fileManager =
  [NSFileManager defaultManager];

NSString *documentsPath =
  [NSSearchPathForDirectoriesInDomains(
    NSDocumentDirectory, NSUserDomainMask, YES)
  firstObject];

NSString *filePath = [documentsPath
  stringByAppendingPathComponent:@"file.txt"];

BOOL fileExists = [fileManager
  fileExistsAtPath:filePath];
```

Listing All Files In A Directory

```
NSFileManager *fileManager =
  [NSFileManager defaultManager];
NSURL *bundleURL = [[NSBundle mainBundle] bundleURL];
NSArray *contents =
  [fileManager contentsOfDirectoryAtURL:bundleURL
            includingPropertiesForKeys:@[]
          options:NSDirectoryEnumerationSkipsHiddenFiles
                            error:nil];

NSPredicate *predicate =
  [NSPredicate predicateWithFormat:
    @"pathExtension ENDSWITH '.png'"];

for (NSString *path in
     [contents filteredArrayUsingPredicate:predicate])
{
    // Enumerate each .png file in directory
}
```

Recursively Enumerating Files In A Directory

```
NSFileManager *fileManager =
  [NSFileManager defaultManager];
NSURL *bundleURL = [[NSBundle mainBundle] bundleURL];


NSDirectoryEnumerator *enumerator =
  [fileManager enumeratorAtURL:bundleURL
    includingPropertiesForKeys:@[NSURLNameKey,
                                 NSURLIsDirectoryKey]
        options:NSDirectoryEnumerationSkipsHiddenFiles
      errorHandler:^BOOL(NSURL *url, NSError *error)
{
    NSLog(@"[Error] %@ (%@)", error, url);
}];


NSMutableArray *mutableFileURLs =
  [NSMutableArray array];


for (NSURL *fileURL in enumerator)
{
    NSString *filename;
    [fileURL getResourceValue:&filename
                       forKey:NSURLNameKey
                        error:nil];


    NSNumber *isDirectory;
    [fileURL getResourceValue:&isDirectory
                       forKey:NSURLIsDirectoryKey
                        error:nil];
```

```
    // Skip directories with '_' prefix, for example
    if ([isDirectory boolValue] &&
        [filename hasPrefix:@"_"])
    {
        [enumerator skipDescendants];
        continue;
    }

    if (![isDirectory boolValue]) {
        [mutableFileURLs addObject:fileURL];
    }
}
```

Creating a Directory

```
NSFileManager *fileManager =
  [NSFileManager defaultManager];
NSString *documentsPath =
  [NSSearchPathForDirectoriesInDomains(
      NSDocumentDirectory, NSUserDomainMask, YES)
    firstObject];

NSString *imagesPath = [documentsPath
    stringByAppendingPathComponent:@"images"];

if (![fileManager fileExistsAtPath:imagesPath])
{
    [fileManager createDirectoryAtPath:imagesPath
            withIntermediateDirectories:NO
                             attributes:nil
                                  error:nil];
}
```

Deleting a File

```objectivec
NSFileManager *fileManager =
  [NSFileManager defaultManager];
NSString *documentsPath =
  [NSSearchPathForDirectoriesInDomains(
      NSDocumentDirectory, NSUserDomainMask, YES)
  firstObject];

NSString *filePath = [documentsPath
  stringByAppendingPathComponent:@"image.png"];

NSError *error = nil;
if (![fileManager removeItemAtPath:filePath
                            error:&error])
{
    NSLog(@"[Error] %@ (%@)", error, filePath);
}
```

Determine the Creation Date of a File

```
NSFileManager *fileManager =
  [NSFileManager defaultManager];
NSString *documentsPath =
  [NSSearchPathForDirectoriesInDomains(
      NSDocumentDirectory, NSUserDomainMask, YES)
  firstObject];

NSString *filePath = [documentsPath
  stringByAppendingPathComponent:@"Document.pages"];

NSDate *creationDate = nil;
if ([fileManager fileExistsAtPath:filePath]) {
    NSDictionary *attributes =
      [fileManager attributesOfItemAtPath:filePath
                                    error:nil];
    creationDate = attributes[NSFileCreationDate];
}
```

There are a number of file attributes that are made accessible through NSFileManager, which can be fetched with -attributesOfItemAtPath:error:, and other methods:

File Attribute Keys

- NSFileAppendOnly: whether the file is read-only.

- NSFileBusy: whether the file is busy.

- NSFileCreationDate: the file's creation date.

- NSFileOwnerAccountName: the name of the file's owner.

- NSFileGroupOwnerAccountName: the group name of the file's owner.

- NSFileDeviceIdentifier: the identifier for the device on which the file resides.

- NSFileExtensionHidden: whether the file's extension is hidden.

- NSFileGroupOwnerAccountID: the file's group ID.

- NSFileHFSCreatorCode: the file's HFS creator code.

- NSFileHFSTypeCode: the file's HFS type code.

- NSFileImmutable: whether the file is mutable.

- NSFileModificationDate: the file's last modified date.

- NSFileOwnerAccountID: the file's owner's account ID.

- NSFilePosixPermissions: the file's Posix permissions.

- NSFileReferenceCount: the file's reference count.

- NSFileSize: the file's size in bytes.

- NSFileSystemFileNumber: the file's filesystem file number.

- NSFileType: the file's type.

NSFileManagerDelegate

NSFileManager may optionally set a delegate to verify that it should perform a particular file operation. This allows the business logic, like which files to protect from deletion, to be factored out of a controller.

There are four kinds of methods in the <NSFileManagerDelegate> protocol, each with a variation for working with paths, as well as methods for error handling.

- -fileManager:shouldMoveItemAtURL:toURL:
- -fileManager:shouldCopyItemAtURL:toURL:
- -fileManager:shouldRemoveItemAtURL:
- -fileManager:shouldLinkItemAtURL:toURL:

Wondering when one might alloc init an NSFileManager, rather than using the shared instance? This is it.

As per the documentation:

> If you use a delegate to receive notifications about the status of move, copy, remove, and link operations, you should create a unique instance of the file manager object, assign your delegate to that object, and use that file manager to initiate your operations.

```objc
NSFileManager *fileManager =
  [[NSFileManager alloc] init];
fileManager.delegate = delegate;

NSURL *bundleURL = [[NSBundle mainBundle] bundleURL];
NSArray *contents = [fileManager
  contentsOfDirectoryAtURL:bundleURL
includingPropertiesForKeys:@[]
         options:NSDirectoryEnumerationSkipsHiddenFiles
           error:nil];

for (NSString *filePath in contents) {
    [fileManager removeItemAtPath:filePath error:nil];
}
```

CustomFileManagerDelegate.m

```objc
#pragma mark - NSFileManagerDelegate

- (BOOL)fileManager:(NSFileManager *)fileManager
shouldRemoveItemAtURL:(NSURL *)URL
{
    // Don't delete PDFs
    return ![[[URL lastPathComponent] pathExtension]
isEqualToString:@"pdf"];
}
```

Ubiquitous Storage

Documents can also be moved to iCloud. If you guessed that this would be anything but straight forward, you'd be 100% correct.

Because URLForUbiquityContainerIdentifier: and setUbiquitous:itemAtURL:destinationURL:error: are blocking calls, this entire operation needs to be dispatched off the main queue.

This is another occasion when one would create a new NSFileManager rather than using the shared instance.

Move Item to Ubiquitous Storage

```
dispatch_async(dispatch_get_global_queue(
            DISPATCH_QUEUE_PRIORITY_BACKGROUND, 0), ^
{
    NSFileManager *fileManager =
      [[NSFileManager alloc] init];
    NSString *documentsPath =
      [NSSearchPathForDirectoriesInDomains(
          NSDocumentDirectory, NSUserDomainMask, YES)
      firstObject];
    NSURL *fileURL =
      [NSURL fileURLWithPath:[documentsPath
      stringByAppendingPathComponent:@"Document.pages"]];
```

```objc
// Defaults to first listed in entitlements if nil
// Should be replaced with real identifier
NSString *identifier = nil;

NSURL *ubiquitousContainerURL = [fileManager
    URLForUbiquityContainerIdentifier:identifier];
NSURL *ubiquitousFileURL = [ubiquitousContainerURL
    URLByAppendingPathComponent:@"Document.pages"];

NSError *error = nil;
BOOL success = [fileManager setUbiquitous:YES
                            itemAtURL:fileURL
                       destinationURL:ubiquitousFileURL
                                error:&error];
if (!success) {
    NSLog(@"[Error] %@ (%@) (%@)", error, fileURL,
ubiquitousFileURL);
    }
});
```

You can find more information about ubiquitous document storage in Apple's "iCloud File Management" document.

There's a lot to know about file systems, but as an app developer, it's mostly an academic exercise. Academic exercises are great, but they don't ship code.

NSFileManager allows you to leave studying for another day, and just get things done.

NSValue

What makes Objective-C such a curiosity is the way it merges the old, procedural world of C with the modern Object-Oriented influences of Smalltalk. When done correctly, this tension can be exploited to craft semantically rich software without sacrificing performance. But bridging that gap between old and new is a miasma of casts, bridges, and boxes.

Boxing is the process of encapsulating scalars (int, double, BOOL, etc.) and value types (struct, enum) inside an object container. It is primarily used to store those values in collection objects.

NSNumber is often used to box scalars, but in Foundation, the reigning featherweight champion of boxing is NSValue.

NSValue is a container for a single C or Objective-C data values. It can hold scalars and value types, as well as pointers and object IDs.

While boxing is an admittedly dry subject matter, there are two methods in particular that are worth calling out: +valueWithBytes:objCType:, which serves as a primer for working with NSValue, and +valueWithNonretainedObject:, which is surprisingly useful, despite being relatively unknown.

valueWithBytes:objCType:

+valueWithBytes:objCType: Creates and returns an NSValue object containing a value of a specified Objective-C type.

- value: the value for the new NSValue object.

- type: the Objective-C type of value. type should be created with the Objective-C @encode() compiler directive; it should not be hard-coded as a C string.

@encode was discussed in the @ Compiler Directives chapter:

- @encode(): returns the type encoding of a type. This type value can be used as the first argument encode in NSCoder -encodeValueOfObjCType:at.

valueWithNonretainedObject:

+valueWithNonretainedObject: Creates and returns an NSValue object that contains a given object.

In short, valueWithNonretainedObject: allows objects to be added to a collection, without the need for satisfying <NSCopying>.

This comes up occasionally when working with objects that can't be directly added to an NSArray or NSDictionary. Without knowing about this method, this break in the abstraction is a show-stopper—especially for anyone just starting out in Objective-C.

Having unpacked all of this wisdom about NSValue, you can now face that cruel divide between procedural and object-oriented; C and Smalltalk.

NSValueTransformer

Of all the Foundation classes, NSValueTransformer is perhaps the one that fared the worst in the shift from OS X to iOS.

Why? Well, there are two reasons:

The first and most obvious reason is that NSValueTransformer was mainly used with Cocoa bindings, to automatically transform values from one property to another without the need of intermediary glue code. iOS, of course, doesn't have bindings.

The second reason has less to do with iOS than Objective-C itself. With the introduction of blocks, it got much easier to pass behavior between objects—significantly easier than, say using NSValueTransformer or NSInvocation. Even if iOS were to get bindings tomorrow, it's uncertain as to whether NSValueTransformer would play a significant role this time around.

But you know what? NSValueTransformer is ripe for a comeback.

With a little bit of re-tooling and some recontextualization, this blast from the past could be the next big thing in your application.

NSValueTransformer is an abstract class that transforms one value into another. A typical implementation would look something like this:

```objc
@interface ClassNameTransformer: NSValueTransformer {}
@end

#pragma mark -

@implementation ClassNameTransformer
+ (Class)transformedValueClass {
  return [NSString class];
}

+ (BOOL)allowsReverseTransformation {
    return NO;
}

- (id)transformedValue:(id)value {
    return (value == nil) ? nil :
NSStringFromClass([value class]);
}

@end
```

NSValueTransformer is rarely initialized directly. Instead, it follows a pattern similar to NSPersistentStore or NSURLProtocol, wherein a class is registered, and instances are created from a manager—except in this case, instances are registered with a particular name:

```
NSString * const ClassNameTransformerName =
  @"ClassNameTransformer";

// Set the value transformer
[NSValueTransformer setValueTransformer:
  [[ClassNameTransformer alloc] init]
                  forName:ClassNameTransformerName];

// Get the value transformer
NSValueTransformer *valueTransformer =
  [NSValueTransformer valueTransformerForName:
    ClassNameTransformerName];
```

Register subclass instances in the +initialize method, so it could be used without any further configuration.

At this point, NSValueTransformer's fatal flaw is abundantly clear: it's a pain in the ass to set up!

Create a class, implement a handful of simple methods, define a constant, and register it in an +initialize method? No thanks.

In this age of blocks, we want—nay, demand—a way to declare functionality in one (albeit gigantic) line of code.

Nothing a little metaprogramming can't fix. Behold:

```
NSString * const TKCapitalizedStringTransformerName =
  @"TKCapitalizedStringTransformerName";

[NSValueTransformer
  registerValueTransformerWithName:
    TKCapitalizedStringTransformerName
            transformedValueClass:[NSString class]
returningTransformedValueWithBlock:^id(id value)
{
  return [value capitalizedString];
}];
```

NSValueTransformer, far from a vestige of AppKit, remains Foundation's purest connection to that mantra of computation: input goes in, output comes out.

Although it hasn't aged very well on its own, a little modernization restores NSValueTransformer to that highest esteem of NSHipsterdom: the solution that we didn't know we needed, but was there all along.

NSDataDetector

Machines speak in binary, while humans speak in riddles, half-truths, and omissions. And until humanity embraces RDF for all of their daily interactions, a large chunk of artificial intelligence is going to go into figuring out what the heck we're all talking about.

In the basic interactions of our daily lives—meeting people, making plans, finding information online—there is immense value in automatically converting from implicit human language to explicit structured data, so that it can be easily added to our calendars, address books, maps, and reminders.

Fortunately for Cocoa developers, there's an easy solution: NSDataDetector.

NSDataDetector is a subclass of NSRegularExpression, but instead of matching on an ICU pattern, it detects semi-structured information: dates, addresses, links, phone numbers and transit information.

It does all of this with frightening accuracy. NSDataDetector will match flight numbers, address snippets, oddly formatted digits, and even relative deictic expressions like "next Saturday at 5".

Think of it as a regexp matcher with incredibly complicated expressions that extract information from natural language (though its actual implementation details may be somewhat more oblique than that).

NSDataDetector objects are initialized with a bitmask of which types of information to check, and then passed strings to match on. Like NSRegularExpression, each match found in a string is represented by a NSTextCheckingResult, which includes details like character range and match type. However, NSDataDetector-specific types may also contain metadata such as address or date components.

```
NSError *error = nil;
NSDataDetector *detector =
  [NSDataDetector dataDetectorWithTypes:
    NSTextCheckingTypeAddress |
    NSTextCheckingTypePhoneNumber
                    error:&error];

NSString *string = @"123 Main St. / (555) 555-5555";
[detector enumerateMatchesInString:string
        options:kNilOptions
          range:NSMakeRange(0, [string length])
      usingBlock:^(NSTextCheckingResult *result,
NSMatchingFlags flags, BOOL *stop)
{
  NSLog(@"Match: %@", result);
}];
```

When initializing NSDataDetector, be sure to specify only the types you're interested in. With each additional type to be checked comes a nontrivial performance cost.

Data Detector Match Types

NSTextCheckingResult is used for many different purposes across Foundation, so it may not be immediately clear which properties are specific to NSDataDetector. Here is a table of the different NSTextCheckingTypes for NSDataDetector matches, and their associated properties:

Type	Properties
NSTextCheckingTypeDate	date duration timeZone
NSTextCheckingTypeAddress	addressComponents* • NSTextCheckingNameKey • NSTextCheckingJobTitleKey • NSTextCheckingOrganizationKey • NSTextCheckingStreetKey • NSTextCheckingCityKey • NSTextCheckingStateKey • NSTextCheckingZIPKey • NSTextCheckingCountryKey • NSTextCheckingPhoneKey
NSTextCheckingTypeLink	url
NSTextCheckingType PhoneNumber	phoneNumber
NSTextCheckingType TransitInformation	components* • NSTextCheckingAirlineKey • NSTextCheckingFlightKey

Data Detection on iOS

Rather confusingly, iOS also defines UIDataDetectorTypes. A bitmask of these values can be set as the dataDetectorTypes of a UITextView to have detected data automatically linked in the displayed text.

UIDataDetectorTypes is distinct from NSTextCheckingTypes. Equivalent enum constants, such as UIDataDetectorTypePhoneNumber and

NSTextCheckingTypePhoneNumber, do not have the same integer value, and not all values in one are found in the other.

Converting from UIDataDetectorTypes to NSTextCheckingTypes can be accomplished with a function:

```
static inline NSTextCheckingType
  NSTextCheckingTypesFromUIDataDetectorTypes(
    UIDataDetectorTypes dataDetectorType)
{
    NSTextCheckingType textCheckingType = 0;
    if (dataDetectorType & UIDataDetectorTypeAddress) {
        textCheckingType |= NSTextCheckingTypeAddress;
    }
    if (dataDetectorType &
UIDataDetectorTypeCalendarEvent) {
        textCheckingType |= NSTextCheckingTypeDate;
    }
    if (dataDetectorType & UIDataDetectorTypeLink) {
        textCheckingType |= NSTextCheckingTypeLink;
    }    if (dataDetectorType &
UIDataDetectorTypePhoneNumber) {
        textCheckingType |=
NSTextCheckingTypePhoneNumber;
    }

    return textCheckingType;
}
```

Do I detect some disbelief of how easy it is to translate between natural language and structured data? This should not be surprising, given how insanely great Cocoa's linguistic APIs are.

Don't make your users re-enter information by hand because of a programming oversight. Take advantage of NSDataDetector in your app to unlock the structure of information.

CFBag

Objective-C is a language caught between two worlds.

On one side, it follows the thoughtful, object-oriented philosophy of Smalltalk, which brings ideas like message sending and named parameters. On the other, are the inescapable vestiges of C, which brings power and a dash of chaos.

It's an identity crisis borne out through the relationship between the Foundation and Core Foundation frameworks, particularly with the toll-free bridged collection class clusters: NSArray / CFArray, NSDictionary / CFDictionary, and NSSet / CFSet. These collections can be passed back and forth between C functions and Objective-C methods without conversion. A leak in the abstraction, but a useful way to optimize the most critical parts of an application nonetheless.

Caught in the middle of this war of abstraction is the least-assuming of all collection types: CFBag.

Foundation	Core Foundation	Toll-Free Bridged
NSArray*	CFArray*	✓
NSCountedSet	CFBag*	
N/A	CFBinaryHeap	
N/A	CFBitVector*	
NSDictionary*	CFDictionary*	✓
NSIndexSet*	N/A	
NSMapTable	N/A	
NSOrderedSet	N/A	
NSPointerArray	N/A	
NSPointerFunctions	N/A	
NSSet*	CFSet*	✓

Take a look at the second row, and note that NSCountedSet and CFBag, unlike the other Foundation / Core Foundation correspondence, are not toll-free bridged. No real explanation for this is provided, aside from it being acknowledged in the NSCountedSet documentation.

Bags, in the Abstract

In the pantheon of collection data types within computer science, bag doesn't really have the same clout as lists, sets, associative arrays, trees, graphs, or priority queues.

In fact, it's pretty obscure. You've probably never heard of it.

A bag, or multi-set, is a variant of a set, where members can appear more than once. A count is associated with each unique member of the collection, representing the number of times it has been added. Like with sets, order does not matter.

Its practical applications are... limited.

Tallying votes in a general election?
Simulating homework problems an intro probability class?
Implementing a game of Yahtzee?

If so, then bag is your new bicycle!

Working with CFMutableBag

As an implementation of the bag data type, CFBag and its mutable counterpart, CFMutableBag, are pretty slick.

Although it lacks the object-oriented convenience of NSCountedSet, CFMutableBag makes up for it with a number of ways to customize its behavior. When a bag is created, it can be initialized with a number of callbacks, which specify the way values are inserted, removed, and compared:

```
struct CFBagCallBacks {
    CFIndex version;
    CFBagRetainCallBack retain;
    CFBagReleaseCallBack release;
    CFBagCopyDescriptionCallBack copyDescription;
    CFBagEqualCallBack equal;
    CFBagHashCallBack
typedef struct CFBagCallBacks CFBagCallBacks;
```

- retain: callback used to retain values as they're added to the collection

- release: callback used to release values as they're removed from the collection

- copyDescription: callback used to create a string description of each value in the collection

- equal: callback used to compare values in the collection for equality

- hash: callback used to compute hash codes for values in the collection

For example, if one were to implement a vote tallying application, one could specify a normalizing function for retain to ensure that votes for mixed-case or misspelled names went to the right candidate... or ensure that the "correct" candidate is shown to be the winner when all the votes are in, with the equal callback.

CFMutableBag also has CFBagApplyFunction, which has the ability to transform values over the collection, to "smooth out" vote counts.

Basically, if you need to rig an election, CFBag is your best bet.

But seriously, CFBag is useful in its own right, and serves as a reminder of the hidden gems to be found within the standard frameworks and libraries.

NSCache

Poor NSCache, always being overshadowed by NSMutableDictionary. It's as if no one knew how it provides all of that garbage collection behavior that developers take great pains to re-implement themselves.

That's right: NSCache is effectively an NSMutableDictionary that automatically evicts objects to free up space in memory as necessary. No need to respond to memory warnings or contrive a cache-clearing timer mechanism. The only other difference is that keys aren't copied as they are in an NSMutableDictionary, which is actually to its advantage (no need for keys to conform to <NSCopying>).

If developers only knew...

But you're not like the others, right?
You won't overlook NSCache, *will you*?

That's not to say that there aren't a few warts and inexplicable caveats—far from it. NSCache is kind of a hot mess.

Take setObject:forKey:cost:, for example. It's the same setObject:forKey: method as before, but with this cost parameter. What is that, you ask? Well, even the documentation isn't quite sure:

> *The cost value is used to compute a sum encompassing the costs of all the objects in the cache. When memory is limited or when the total cost of the cache eclipses the maximum allowed total cost, the cache could begin an eviction process to remove some of its elements.*

Alright, so far so good...

> *However, this eviction process is not in a guaranteed order. As a consequence, if you try to manipulate the cost values to achieve some specific behavior, the consequences could be detrimental to your program.*

Huh? So what's the point, then?

> *Typically, the obvious cost is the size of the value in bytes. If that information is not readily available, you should not go through the trouble of trying to compute it, as doing so will drive up the cost of using the cache.*

So wait, what's a non-obvious cost value? Any guidelines for what a memory limit should be? Order of magnitude, even? "Arbitrarily guess wrong and suffer bad performance" doesn't sound so compelling...

Pass in 0 for the cost value if you otherwise have nothing useful to pass, or simply use the setObject:forKey: method, which does not require a cost value to be passed in.

Read: don't use this method unless you work at Apple and know the original author personally.

There's also a whole section about controlling whether objects are automatically evicted with evictsObjectsWithDiscardedContent & <NSDiscardableContent>, but it will probably just cause heartache and sorrow.

Despite all of this, developers should be using NSCache a lot more than they currently are. Anything in a project named "cache" that isn't NSCache would be ripe for replacement. Just be sure to stick to the basics: objectForKey:, setObject:forKey: & removeObjectForKey:.

NSIndexSet

NSIndexSet is a sorted collection of unique unsigned integers. Think of it like an NSRange that supports non-contiguous series. It has wicked fast operations for set intersections, and comes with all of the convenience methods you'd expect in a Foundation collection class.

It's used throughout the Foundation framework, whenever a method gets multiple elements from a sorted collection, such as an array or a table view's data source.

Squint hard enough, and aspects of a data model may start to look NSIndexSet-shaped. For example, an index set could be used to represent HTTP response status codes, such that "acceptable" codes (in the 2XX range), can be checked with containsIndex:.

Here are a couple more ideas:

- Have a list of user preferences, and want to store which ones are switched on or off? Use a single NSIndexSet in combination with an enum typedef.

- Filtering a list of items by a set of composable conditions? Ditch the NSPredicate; instead, cache the indexes of objects that fulfill each condition, and then get the union or intersection of those indexes as conditions are added and removed.

Overall, NSIndexSet is a solid class. A fair bit nerdier than its collection class siblings, but it has its place. At the very least, it's a prime example of the great functionality to be discovered by paying attention to what Foundation uses in its own APIs.

NSOrderedSet

Why isn't NSOrderedSet a subclass of NSSet?

It seems perfectly logical, after all, for NSOrderedSet—a class that enforces the same uniqueness constraint of NSSet—to be a subclass of NSSet. It has the same methods as NSSet, with the addition of some NSArray-style methods like objectAtIndex:. By all accounts, it would seem to perfectly satisfy the requirements of the Liskov substitution principle, that:

> *If S is a subtype of T, then objects of type T in a program may be replaced with objects of type S without altering any of the desirable properties of that program.*

So why is NSOrderedSet a subclass of NSObject and not NSSet or even NSArray?

To answer this, one must understand class clusters.

Mutable / Immutable Class Clusters

Class Clusters are a design pattern at the heart of the Foundation framework; the essence of Objective-C's simplicity in everyday use.

But class clusters offer simplicity at the expense of extensibility, which becomes especially tricky when it comes to mutable / immutable class pairs like NSSet / NSMutableSet.

The method -mutableCopy creates an inconsistency that is inherent to Objective-C's constraint on single inheritance.

Here's how -mutableCopy is supposed to work in a class cluster:

```
NSSet* immutable = [NSSet set];
NSMutableSet* mutable = [immutable mutableCopy];
[mutable isKindOfClass:[NSSet class]]; // YES
[mutable isKindOfClass:[NSMutableSet class]]; // YES
```

Suppose that NSOrderedSet was indeed a subclass of NSSet:

```
// @interface NSOrderedSet : NSSet
NSOrderedSet* immutable = [NSOrderedSet orderedSet];
NSMutableOrderedSet* mutable = [immutable mutableCopy];
[mutable isKindOfClass:[NSSet class]]; // YES
[mutable isKindOfClass:[NSMutableSet class]]; // NO (!)
```

That's no good, since NSMutableOrderedSet couldn't be used as a method parameter of type NSMutableSet.

So what happens if NSMutableOrderedSet is made a subclass of NSMutableSet as well?

```
// @interface NSOrderedSet : NSSet
// @interface NSMutableOrderedSet : NSMutableSet

NSOrderedSet* immutable = [NSOrderedSet orderedSet];
NSMutableOrderedSet* mutable = [immutable mutableCopy];
[mutable isKindOfClass:[NSSet class]]; // YES
[mutable isKindOfClass:[NSMutableSet class]]; // YES
[mutable isKindOfClass:[NSOrderedSet class]]; // NO (!)
```

This is perhaps even worse, as now NSMutableOrderedSet couldn't be used as a method parameter expecting an NSOrderedSet.

No matter how one approaches it, a mutable / immutable class pair can't be stacked on top of another existing mutable / immutable class pair. It just won't work in Objective-C.

Protocols offer a way to get us out of this pickle. Indeed, Foundation's collection classes could become more aspect-oriented by adding protocols:

- NSArray : NSObject <NSOrderedCollection>

- NSSet : NSObject <NSUniqueCollection>

- NSOrderedSet : NSObject
  <NSOrderedCollection, NSUniqueCollection>

However, to reap any benefit from this arrangement, all of the existing APIs would have to be restructured to have parameters accept id <NSOrderedCollection> instead of NSArray. However, the transition would be painful, and would likely open up a whole can of edge cases... which would mean that it would never be fully adopted... which would mean that there's less incentive for developers to adopt this approach when defining your own APIs... which are less fun to write because there's now two incompatible ways to do something instead of one... which...

...wait, why would anyone use NSOrderedSet in the first place, anyway?

NSOrderedSet was introduced in iOS 5 & Mac OS X 10.7. The only APIs changed to add support for NSOrderedSet, though, were part of Core Data.

This was fantastic news for anyone using Core Data at the time, as it solved one of the long-standing annoyances of not having a way to arbitrarily order relationship collections. Previously, one would have to add a position attribute, which would be re-calculated every time a collection was modified. There wasn't a built-in way to validate that your collection positions were unique or that the sequence didn't have any gaps.

In this way, NSOrderedSet is the class everyone had been waiting for.

Unfortunately, its very existence in Foundation creates something between an attractive nuisance and a red herring for API designers.

Although it is perfectly suited to that one particular use case in Core Data, NSOrderedSet is probably not a great choice for the majority of APIs that might use it. In cases where a simple collection of objects is passed as a parameter, a simple NSArray does the trick. If uniqueness does matter, or the semantics of sets makes sense for a particular method, NSSet has and remains a great choice.

So, as a general rule: NSOrderedSet is useful for intermediary and internal representations, but one probably shouldn't introduce it as a method parameter unless it's particularly well-suited to the semantics of the data model.

If nothing else, NSOrderedSet illuminates some of the fascinating implications of Foundation's use of the class cluster design pattern. Investigating these implications allows us better understand the trade-off between simplicity and extensibility as we make these choices in our own application designs.

NSHashTable & NSMapTable

NSSet and NSDictionary, along with NSArray are the workhorse collection classes of Foundation. Unlike other standard libraries, implementation details are hidden from developers, allowing them to write simple code and trust that it will be (reasonably) performant.

However, even the best abstractions break down; their underlying assumptions overturned. In these cases, developers either venture further down the abstraction, or, if available use a more general-purpose solution.

For NSSet and NSDictionary, a common breaking assumption is how memory is managed when storing objects in the collection. For NSSet, objects are a strongly referenced, as are NSDictionary values. Keys, on the other hand, are copied by NSDictionary.

If a developer wants to store a weak value, or use a non-<NSCopying>-conforming object as a key, they could be clever and use NSValue +valueWithNonretainedObject. Or, as of iOS 6 (and as far back as Mac OS X 10.5), one could use NSHashTable or NSMapTable—the more general-case counterparts to NSSet or NSDictionary, respectively.

NSHashTable

NSHashTable is a general-purpose analogue of NSSet. Contrasted with the behavior of NSSet / NSMutableSet, NSHashTable has the following characteristics:

- NSSet / NSMutableSet holds strong references to members, which are tested for hashing and equality using the methods hash and isEqual:.

- NSHashTable is mutable, without an immutable counterpart.

- NSHashTable can hold weak references to its members.

- NSHashTable can optionally copy members on input.

- NSHashTable can contain arbitrary pointers, and use pointer identity for equality and hashing checks.

Usage

Instances where one might use NSHashTable include storing weak objects or copies.

```
NSHashTable *hashTable = [NSHashTable
hashTableWithOptions:NSPointerFunctionsCopyIn];
[hashTable addObject:@"foo"];
[hashTable addObject:@"bar"];
[hashTable addObject:@42];
[hashTable removeObject:@"bar"];
NSLog(@"Members: %@", [hashTable allObjects]);
```

NSHashTable objects are initialized with an option for any of the following behaviors:

- NSHashTableStrongMemory: equal to NSPointerFunctionsStrongMemory. This is default behavior, equivalent to NSSet member storage.

- NSHashTableWeakMemory: equal to NSPointerFunctionsWeakMemory. Uses weak read and write barriers. Using NSPointerFunctionsWeakMemory object references will turn to NULL on last release.

- NSHashTableZeroingWeakMemory: this option has been deprecated. Instead use the NSHashTableWeakMemory option.

- NSHashTableCopyIn: use the memory acquire function to allocate and copy items on input (see NSPointerFunction - acquireFunction). Equal to NSPointerFunctionsCopyIn.

- NSHashTableObjectPointerPersonality: use shifted pointer for the hash value and direct comparison to determine equality; use the description method for a description. Equal to NSPointerFunctionsObjectPointerPersonality.

Deprecated enum values are due to NSHashTable being ported from Garbage-Collected Mac OS X to ARC-ified iOS.

NSMapTable

NSMapTable is a general-purpose analogue of NSDictionary. Contrasted with the behavior of NSDictionary / NSMutableDictionary, NSMapTable has the following characteristics:

- NSDictionary / NSMutableDictionary copies keys, and holds strong references to values.

- NSMapTable is mutable, without an immutable counterpart.

- NSMapTable can hold keys and values with weak references, in such a way that entries are removed when either the key or value is deallocated.

- NSMapTable can optionally copy its values on input.

- NSMapTable can contain arbitrary pointers, and use pointer identity for equality and hashing checks.

Usage

Instances where one might use NSMapTable include non-copyable keys and storing weak references to keyed delegates or another kind of weak object.

```
id delegate = ...;
NSMapTable *mapTable = [NSMapTable
mapTableWithKeyOptions:NSMapTableStrongMemory

valueOptions:NSMapTableWeakMemory];
[mapTable setObject:delegate forKey:@"foo"];
NSLog(@"Keys: %@", [[mapTable keyEnumerator]
allObjects]);
```

NSMapTable objects are initialized with options specifying behavior for both keys and values, using the following enum values:

- NSMapTableStrongMemory: Specifies a strong reference from the map table to its contents.

- NSMapTableWeakMemory: Uses weak read and write barriers appropriate for ARC or GC. Using NSPointerFunctionsWeakMemory object references will turn to NULL on last release. Equal to NSMapTableZeroingWeakMemory.

- NSHashTableZeroingWeakMemory: This option has been superseded by the NSMapTableWeakMemory option.

- NSMapTableCopyIn Use the memory acquire function to allocate and copy items on input (see acquireFunction (see NSPointerFunction -acquireFunction). Equal to NSPointerFunctionsCopyIn.

- NSMapTableObjectPointerPersonality: Use shifted pointer hash and direct equality, object description. Equal to NSPointerFunctionsObjectPointerPersonality.

Subscripting

After looking at a few code examples, clever readers may have thought "why aren't we using object subscripting?". Particularly enterprising readers may have even gotten a few lines of code into implementing a subscripting category for NSMapTable!

So why doesn't NSMapTable implement subscripting? Take a look at these method signatures:

```
- (id)objectForKeyedSubscript:(id <NSCopying>)key;
- (void)setObject:(id)obj
forKeyedSubscript:(id <NSCopying>)key;
```

Notice that the key argument is of type <NSCopying>. This is great for NSDictionary NSMutableDictionary, but the same assumption can't be made for NSMapTable.

And so we arrive at an impasse: with an id <NSCopying> type, we can't implement for NSMapTable. However, if object subscripting methods were to drop the <NSCopying> constraint, then we'd miss out on the compiler check in NSMutableDictionary -setObject:forKeyedSubscript:.

So it goes. Honestly, in a situation where NSMapTable is merited, syntactic sugar is probably the least of one's concerns.

As always, it's important to remember that programming is not about being cleve. One should always approach a problem from the highest viable level of abstraction.

NSSet and NSDictionary are great classes; for 99% of situations, they are undoubtedly the correct tool for the job. If, however, your problem has any of the particular memory management constraints described above, then NSHashTable & NSMapTable may be worth a look.

UIKit

UIMenuController

Mobile usability today is remarkable—especially considering how far it's come in just the last decade.

What was once a clumsy technology relegated to the tech elite has now become the primary mode of computation for the general population.

Yet despite its advances, one can't help but feel occasionally... trapped.

All too often, there will be information on the screen that you just can't access. Whether its flight information stuck in a table view cell or an unlinked URL, users are forced to solve problems creatively for lack of a provided solution.

What's crazy is that iOS provides that solution with UIMenuController and edit actions, and still, very few developers take advantage of it. By the end of this chapter, you'll have all of the knowledge and wherewithal to be the change mobile usability so desperately craves.

Copy, Cut, Paste, Delete, Select

iOS 3's killer feature was undoubtedly push notifications, but the ability to copy-paste is a close second. For how much it's used everyday, it's difficult to imagine how anyone got along without it. And yet, it remains a relatively obscure feature for 3rd-party apps.

This may be due to how cumbersome it is to implement:

HipsterLabel.{h,m}

```
@interface HipsterLabel : UILabel
@end

@implementation HipsterLabel
- (BOOL)canBecomeFirstResponder {
    return YES;
}
- (BOOL)canPerformAction:(SEL)action
            withSender:(id)sender {
    return (action == @selector(copy:));
}
#pragma mark - UIResponderStandardEditActions
- (void)copy:(id)sender {
  [[UIPasteboard generalPasteboard] setString:self.text];
}
@end
```

ViewController.m

```objc
- (void)viewDidLoad {
    HipsterLabel *label = ...;
    label.userInteractionEnabled = YES;
    [self.view addSubview:label];

    UIGestureRecognizer *gestureRecognizer =
[[UILongPressGestureRecognizer alloc]
initWithTarget:self
action:@selector(handleLongPressGesture:)];
    [label addGestureRecognizer:gestureRecognizer];
}


#pragma mark - UIGestureRecognizer

- (void)handleLongPressGesture:(UIGestureRecognizer
*)recognizer  {
    UIMenuController *menuController = [UIMenuController
sharedMenuController];
    [menuController setTargetRect:recognizer.view.frame
inView:recognizer.view.superview];
    [menuController setMenuVisible:YES animated:YES];

    [recognizer.view becomeFirstResponder];
}
```

Just to be clear—in order to allow a label's text to be copied, the following must happen:

- UILabel must be subclassed to implement canBecomeFirstResponder & canPerformAction:withSender:

- Each performable action must implement a corresponding method that interacts with UIPasteboard

- When instantiated by a controller, the label must have userInteractionEnabled set to YES (it is not recommended that this be hard-coded into the subclass implementation)

- A UIGestureRecognizer must be added to the label, or UIResponder methods must be implemented.

- In the method implementation corresponding to the gesture recognizer action, UIMenuController must be positioned and made visible

- Finally, the label must become first responder

Why, oh why, isn't this just built into UILabel? That's a *very* good question.

UIMenuController

UIMenuController is responsible for presenting menu items for edit action. Each app has its own singleton instance, sharedMenuController.

By default, a menu controller will show commands for any methods in the UIResponderStandardEditActions informal protocol for which the responder returns YES in canPerformAction:withSender:.

Handling Copy, Cut, Delete, and Paste Commands

Each command travels from the first responder up the responder chain until it is handled. If a responder doesn't handle the command in the current context, it should be passed to the next responder. It is ignored if no responder handles it

- copy: This method is invoked when the user taps the Copy command of the editing menu. Using the methods of the UIPasteboard class, it should convert the selection into an appropriate object (if necessary) and write that object to a pasteboard.

- cut: This method is invoked when the user taps the Cut command of the editing menu. Using the methods of the UIPasteboard class, it should convert the selection into an appropriate object (if necessary) and write that object to a pasteboard. It should also remove the selected object from the user interface and, if applicable, from the application's data model.

- delete: This method is invoked when the user taps the Delete command of the editing menu. This is typically implemented by removing the selected object from the user interface and, if applicable, from the application's data model. It should not write any data to the pasteboard.

- paste: This method is invoked when the user taps the Paste command of the editing menu. Using the methods of the UIPasteboard class, it should read the data in the pasteboard, convert the data into an appropriate internal representation (if necessary), and display it in the user interface.

Handling Selection Commands

- select: This method is invoked when the user taps the Select command of the editing menu. This command is used for targeted selection of items in the receiving view that can be broken up into chunks. This could be, for example, words in a text view. Another example might be a view that puts lists of visible objects in multiple groups; the select: command could be implemented to select all the items in the same group as the currently selected item.

- selectAll: This method is invoked when the user taps the Select All command of the editing menu.

In addition to these basic editing commands, there are commands that deal with rich text editing (toggleBoldface:, toggleItalics:, and toggleUnderline:) and writing direction changes (makeTextWritingDirectionLeftToLeft: & makeTextWritingDirectionLeftToRight:).

UIMenuItem

As of iOS 3.2, developers can add their own commands to the menu controller. Familiar, but as-yet-unmentioned commands like "Define" or spell check suggestions take advantage of this.

UIMenuController has a menuItems property, which is an NSArray of UIMenuItem objects. Each UIMenuItem object has a title and action. In order to have a menu item command display in a menu controller, the responder must implement the corresponding selector.

Just as a skilled coder designs software to be flexible and adaptable to unforeseen use cases, any app developer worth their salt understands the need to accommodate users with different needs from themselves.

Take to heart the following guidelines:

- For every control, think about what a user would expect a right-click (control-click) to do if used from the desktop.

- Any time information is shown to the user, consider whether it should be copyable.

- With formatted or multi-faceted information, consider whether multiple kinds of copy commands are appropriate.

- When implementing copy: make sure to copy only valuable information to the pasteboard.

- For editable controls, ensure that your implementation paste: can handle a wide range of valid and invalid input.

If mobile is to become the dominant computing paradigm, the least we can do is make our best effort to allow users to be more productive. Your thoughtful use of UIMenuController will not go unnoticed.

UILocalizedIndexedCollation

UITableView starts to become unwieldy after a few hundred rows. If users are reduced to frantically scratching at the screen like a cat playing Fruit Ninja in order to get at what they want... one may want to rethink your UI approach.

So, what are the options?

Data could be organized into a hierarchy, which could dramatically reduce the number of rows displayed on each screen in fashion, based on its branching factor.

A UISearchBar could be added to the top of the table view, allowing users to filter on keywords to get exactly what they're looking for.

There is also a third approach, which is woefully under-utilized in iOS applications: section index titles. These are the vertically flowing letters found along the right side of table views in an Address Book contacts list or Music library.

As the user scrolls their finger down the list, the table view jumps to the corresponding section. Even the most tiresome table view is rendered significantly more usable as a result.

Section index titles can be enabled by implementing the following UITableViewDataSource delegate methods:

- -sectionIndexTitlesForTableView: - Returns an array of the section index titles to be displayed along the right hand side of the table view, such as the alphabetical list "A...Z" + "#". Section index titles are short—generally limited to 2 Unicode characters.

- -tableView:sectionForSectionIndexTitle:atIndex: - Returns the section index that the table view should jump to when the user touches a particular section index title.

However, the process of generating that alphabetical list is not something that one would want to have to generate themselves. What it means for something to be alphabetically sorted, or even what is meant by an "alphabet" varies wildly across different languages and locales.

Coming to the rescue is UILocalizedIndexedCollation.

UILocalizedIndexedCollation is a class that helps to organize table view sections in a locale-aware manner. Rather than creating the object directly, a shared instance corresponding to the current locale is accessed, with UILocalizedIndexedCollation +currentCollation

The first task for UILocalizedIndexedCollation is to determine which section index titles to display for the current locale, which are can be read from the sectionIndexTitles property.

Here's an example of how index titles vary between locales:

Locale	Section Index Titles
en_US	A, B, C, D, E, F, G, H, I, J, K, L, M, N, O, P, Q, R, S, T, U, V, W, X, Y, Z, #
ja_JP	A, B, C, D, E, F, G, H, I, J, K, L, M, N, O, P, Q, R, S, T, U, V, W, X, Y, Z, あ, か, さ, た, な, は, ま, や, ら, わ, #
sv_SE	A, B, C, D, E, F, G, H, I, J, K, L, M, N, O, P, Q, R, S, T, U, V, W, X, Y, Z, Å, Ä, Ö, #
ko_KO	A, B, C, D, E, F, G, H, I, J, K, L, M, N, O, P, Q, R, S, T, U, V, W, X, Y, Z, ㄱ, ㄴ, ㄷ, ㄹ, ㅁ, ㅂ, ㅅ, ㅇ, ㅈ, ㅊ, ㅋ, ㅌ, ㅍ, ㅎ, #
ar_SA	A, B, C, D, E, F, G, H, I, J, K, L, M, N, O, P, Q, R, S, T, U, V, W, X, Y, Z, آ, ب, ت, ث, ج, ح, خ, د, ذ, ر, ز, س, ش, ص, ض, ط, ظ, ع, غ, ف, ق, ك, ل, م, ن, ه, و, ي, #

Aren't you glad you don't have to do this yourself?

The next step is to determine what section index each object should be assigned to. This is accomplished with -sectionForObject:collationStringSelector:, which returns the NSInteger index corresponding to the string derived by performing the specified selector. This selector might be something like localizedName, title, or even description.

So, as it stands, a table view data source has a NSArray property corresponding to the number of sections in the table view, with each element of the array containing an array representing each row in the section. Since collation was handled by UILocalizedIndexedCollation, it should be able to sort the rows in each section as well. -sortedArrayFromArray:collationStringSelector: does this in similar fashion to -sectionForObject:collationStringSelector:, sorting objects in each section by their respective localized title.

Finally, the table view should implement -tableView:sectionForSectionIndexTitle:atIndex:, so that touching a section index title jumps to the corresponding section in the table view. UILocalizedIndexedCollation -sectionForSectionIndexTitleAtIndex: does the trick.

All told, here's what a typical table view data source implementation looks like:

```objc
- (void)setObjects:(NSArray *)objects {
    SEL selector = @selector(localizedTitle)
    NSInteger index, sectionTitlesCount =
[[[UILocalizedIndexedCollation currentCollation]
sectionTitles] count];

    NSMutableArray *mutableSections = [[NSMutableArray
alloc] initWithCapacity:sectionTitlesCount];
        for (idx = 0; idx < sectionTitlesCount; idx++) {
            [mutableSections addObject:[NSArray array]];
        }

        for (id object in objects) {
            NSInteger sectionNumber =
[[UILocalizedIndexedCollation currentCollation]
sectionForObject:object
collationStringSelector:selector];
            [[mutableSections objectAtIndex:sectionNumber]
addObject:object];
        }

for (idx = 0; idx < sectionTitlesCount; idx++) {
        NSArray *objectsForSection = [mutableSections
objectAtIndex:idx];
        [mutableSections replaceObjectAtIndex:idx
withObject:[collation
sortedArrayFromArray:objectsForSection
collationStringSelector:selector]];
    }
    self.sections = mutableSections;
    [self.tableView reloadData];
}
```

```objc
- (NSString *)tableView:(UITableView *)tableView
titleForHeaderInSection:(NSInteger)section
{
    return [[[UILocalizedIndexedCollation
currentCollation] sectionTitles] objectAtIndex:section];
}


- (NSArray *)sectionIndexTitlesForTableView:(UITableView
*)tableView {
    return [[UILocalizedIndexedCollation
currentCollation] sectionIndexTitles];
}


- (NSInteger)tableView:(UITableView *)tableView
sectionForSectionIndexTitle:(NSString *)title
              atIndex:(NSInteger)index
{
    return [[UILocalizedIndexedCollation
currentCollation]
sectionForSectionIndexTitleAtIndex:index];
}
```

UITableViewIndexSearch

There is one special section index title worth mentioning, and that's UITableViewIndexSearch. It's common to have both a search bar and section indexes. For convenience and visual consistency, a search icon is usually included as the first section index title. Touching it brings up the UISearchBar in the header of the table view.

To add the search icon in a table view, simply prepend the NSString constant UITableViewIndexSearch to the return value of -sectionIndexTitlesForTableView:, and adjust -tableView:sectionForSectionIndexTitle:atIndex: to account for the single element shift.

If you see an excessively long table view, kill it with fire!

Which is to say, refactor unwieldily content with a combination of hierarchies, a search bar, and section indexes. And when implementing section index titles, take advantage of UILocalizedIndexedCollation.

Together, we can put an end to scroll view-induced repetitive stress injuries, and spend more time enjoying the finer things in life... like watching videos of pets playing with iPads.

UIAppearance

Style vs. Substance.
Message vs. Medium.
Rhetoric vs. Dialectic.

Is beauty merely skin deep,
or is it somehow informed by deeper truths?
What does it mean for something to possess good design?
Are aesthetic judgments relative or absolute?

These are deep questions that have been pondered by philosophers, artists, and makers for millennia.

And while we all continue our search for beauty and understanding in the universe, the app marketplace has been rather clear on this subject:

Users will pay a premium for good-looking software.

When someone purchases an iPhone, they are buying into Apple's philosophy: what works well should look good, too.

It used to be that even trivial UI customization on iOS required AppStore-approval-process-taunting juju like method swizzling. Fortunately, with iOS 5, developers are given an easier way: UIAppearance.

UIAppearance allows the appearance of views and controls to be consistently customized across the entire application.

In order to have this work within the existing structure of UIKit, Apple devised a rather clever solution: UIAppearance is a protocol that returns a proxy which forwards any configuration to every instance of a particular class.

Why a proxy instead of a property or method on UIView directly? Because there are non-UIView objects like UIBarButtonItem that render their own composite views.

Appearance can be customized for all instances, or scoped to particular view hierarchies:

- +appearance: Returns an appearance proxy for the receiver.

- +appearanceWhenContainedIn:(Class <UIAppearanceContainer>)ContainerClass,...: Returns an appearance proxy for the receiver in a given containment hierarchy.

To customize the appearance of all instances of a class, you use appearance to get the appearance proxy for the class. For example, to modify the tint color for all instances of UINavigationBar:

```
[[UINavigationBar appearance] setTintColor:myColor];
```

To customize the appearances in a way that adjusts for being contained within an instance of a container class, or instances in a hierarchy, you use appearanceWhenContainedIn: to get the appearance proxy for the class:

```
[[UIBarButtonItem appearanceWhenContainedIn:
[UINavigationBar class], nil]
        setTintColor:myNavBarColor];
[[UIBarButtonItem appearanceWhenContainedIn:
  [UINavigationBar class], nil]
  setTintColor:myPopoverNavBarColor];
[[UIBarButtonItem appearanceWhenContainedIn:
  [UIToolbar class], nil] setTintColor:myToolbarColor];
[[UIBarButtonItem appearanceWhenContainedIn:
  [UIToolbar class], [UIPopoverController class], nil]
  setTintColor:myPopoverToolbarColor];
```

Determining Which Properties Work With UIAppearance

The major downside to UIAppearance's proxy approach is that it's difficult to determine which selectors are compatible. Because +appearance returns an id, Xcode can't provide any code-completion information. This is a major source of confusion and frustration with this feature.

In order to find out what methods work with UIAppearance, one is forced to grep through the headers:

```
$ cd /Applications/Xcode.app/Contents/Developer/
Platforms/iPhoneOS.platform/Developer/SDKs/
iPhoneOS*.sdk/System/Library/Frameworks/UIKit.framework/
Headers
$ grep -H UI_APPEARANCE_SELECTOR ./* | sed 's/
__OSX_AVAILABLE_STARTING(__MAC_NA,__IPHONE_5_0)
UI_APPEARANCE_SELECTOR;//'
```

UIAppearance looks for the UI_APPEARANCE_SELECTOR macro in method signatures. Any method with this annotation can be used with the appearance proxy.

Implementing <UIAppearance> in Custom UIView Subclasses

Having custom UI classes conform to UIAppearance is not only a best-practice, but it demonstrates a certain level of care being put into its implementation.

Cocoa developers have a long history of obsessing about visual aesthetics—often going to extreme lengths to achieve their desired effects. Recall the Delicious Generation of Mac developers, and applications like Disco, which went so far as to emit virtual smoke when burning a disc.

Thankfully, this obsession for making things look good is alive and well in iOS. As a community and ecosystem, we have relentlessly pushed the envelope in terms of what users should expect from their apps. And though this makes our jobs more challenging, it ultimately makes the experience of developing for iOS all the more enjoyable.

Settle for nothing less than the whole package.
Make your apps beautiful from interface to implementation.

Localization, Internationalization & Accessibility

NSLocale

Internationalization is like flossing: everyone knows they should do it, but probably don't.

And like any habit, it becomes second-nature with practice, to the point that you couldn't imagine not doing it. All it takes is for someone to show you the way.

i18n versus l10n

As is necessary in any discussion about Internationalization (i18n) or Localization (l10n), we must take some time to differentiate the two:

- Localization is the process of adapting your application for a specific market, or locale.

- Internationalization is the process of preparing your app to be localized.

Therefore, internationalization is a necessary, but not sufficient condition for localization.

What makes internationalization difficult is having to think outside of your cultural context. All of the assumptions you have about the way things are supposed to work must be acknowledged and reconsidered. You have to fight the urge to write off things that may seem trivial, like sorting and collation, and empathize with the pain and confusion even minor differences may cause.

Fortunately for us, we don't have to do this alone.
Meet NSLocale:

NSLocale

NSLocale is a Foundation class that encapsulates cultural and linguistic conventions for a particular locale, including:

- Language
- Keyboards
- Number, Date, and Time Formats
- Currency
- Collation and Sorting
- Use of Symbols, Colors, and Iconography

Each locale corresponds to a locale identifier, such as en_US, fr_FR, ja_JP, and en_GB, which include a language code (e.g. en for English) and a region code (e.g. US for United States).

Locale identifiers can encode more explicit preferences for currency, calendar system, or number formats, such as in the case of de_DE@collation=phonebook,currency=DDM, which specifies German spoken in Germany, using phonebook collation, and using the pre-Euro Deutsche Mark.

Users can change their locale settings in the "Langauge & Text" System Preferences on the Mac, or "General > International" in iOS Settings.

-objectForKey:

NSLocale typifies Foundation's obsession with domain-specific pedantry, and nowhere is this more visible than in -objectForKey:.

Among the available values are:

- NSLocaleIdentifier
- NSLocaleLanguageCode
- NSLocaleCountryCode
- NSLocaleScriptCode
- NSLocaleVariantCode
- NSLocaleExemplarCharacterSet
- NSLocaleCalendar

- NSLocaleCollationIdentifier

- NSLocaleUsesMetricSystem

- NSLocaleMeasurementSystem

- NSLocaleDecimalSeparator

- NSLocaleGroupingSeparator

- NSLocaleCurrencySymbol

- NSLocaleCurrencyCode

- NSLocaleCollatorIdentifier

- NSLocaleQuotationBeginDelimiterKey

- NSLocaleQuotationEndDelimiterKey

- NSLocaleAlternateQuotationBeginDelimiterKey

- NSLocaleAlternateQuotationEndDelimiterKey

While this all may seem fairly esoteric, one may be surprised by the number of opportunities an application has to use this information to improve user experience.

It's the small things, like knowing that quotation marks vary between locales:

English	"I can eat glass, it doesn't harm me."
German	„Ich kann Glas essen, das tut mir nicht weh."
Japanese	「私はガラスを食べられます。それは私を傷つけません。」

So, if one were building a component that added quotations around arbitrary text, they should use NSLocaleQuotationBeginDelimiterKey and NSLocaleAlternateQuotationEndDelimiterKey rather than hard-coding English quotation marks (@"\"").

-displayNameForKey:value:

Another impressive method is -displayNameForKey:value:, which can return the display name of a locale identifier (NSLocaleIdentifier):

```
NSLocale *frLocale = [[NSLocale alloc]
    initWithLocaleIdentifier:@"fr_FR"];
NSLog(@"fr_FR: %@", [frLocale
    displayNameForKey:NSLocaleIdentifier value:@"fr_FR"]);
// frFR: français (France)

NSLog(@"en_US: %@", [frLocale
    displayNameForKey:NSLocaleIdentifier value:@"en_US"]);
// enUS: anglais (États-Unis)
```

One should use this method any time information about the user's current or available locales is displayed

+preferredLanguages

One final method worth mentioning is NSLocale +preferredLanguages, which returns an array of IETF BCP 47 language identifiers, in order of user preference.

An app that communicates with a web server can use these values to define the Accept-Language HTTP header, such that the server has the option to return localized resources:

```
NSMutableURLRequest *request = ...;
[request setValue:[NSString stringWithFormat:@"%@",
[[NSLocale preferredLanguages]
componentsJoinedByString:@", "]],
forHTTPHeaderField:@"Accept-Language"];
```

Even if a server doesn't yet localize its resources, putting this in place now will allow it to be changed with the flip the switch—no update to the client required!

Internationalization is often considered to be an un-sexy topic in programming—just another chore that most projects don't have to worry about. In actuality, designing software for other locales is a valuable exercise, and not just for the economic benefits of expanding your software into other markets.

One of the greatest joys and challenges in programming is in designing systems that can withstand change. The only way designs can adapt is by identifying and refactoring assumptions about the system that may not always hold.

In this way, internationalization represents the greatest challenge, making us question everything about our own cultural identity. And in doing so, we become not just better programmers, but better people, too.

So go and be a better person: make NSLocale part of your daily ritual.

NSLocalizedString

Strings are perhaps the most versatile data type in computing. They're passed around as symbols, used to encode numeric values, associate values to keys, represent resource paths, store linguistic content, and format information.

Having a strong handle on user-facing strings, in particular, is essential to making a great user experience. In Foundation, there is a convenient macro for denoting strings as user-facing: NSLocalizedString.

NSLocalizedString provides string localization in "compile-once / run everywhere" fashion, replacing all localized strings with their respective translation at runtime.

NSLocalizedString takes two arguments: key, which uniquely identifies the string to be localized, and comment, a string that is used to provide sufficient context for accurate translation.

In practice, the key is often just the base translation string to be used, while comment is usually nil, unless there is an ambiguous context:

```
textField.placeholder = NSLocalizedString(@"User", nil);
```

NSLocalizedString can also be used as a format string in NSString +stringWithFormat:. In these cases, it's important to use the comment argument to provide enough context to be properly translated.

```
self.title =
  [NSString stringWithFormat:NSLocalizedString(
    @"%@'s Profile",
    @"{User First Name}'s Profile"),
  user.name];
label.text =
  [NSString stringWithFormat:NSLocalizedString(
    @"Showing %lu of %lu items",
    @"Showing {number} of {total number} items"),
  [page count], [items count]];
```

NSLocalizedString & Co.

There are four varieties of NSLocalizedString, with increasing levels of control (and obscurity):

```
NSString * NSLocalizedString(
  NSString *key,
  NSString *comment
)
```

```
NSString * NSLocalizedStringFromTable(
  NSString *key,
  NSString *tableName,
  NSString *comment
)

NSString * NSLocalizedStringFromTableInBundle(
  NSString *key,
  NSString *tableName,
  NSBundle *bundle,
  NSString *comment
)

NSString * NSLocalizedStringWithDefaultValue(
  NSString *key,
  NSString *tableName,
  NSBundle *bundle,
  NSString *value,
  NSString *comment
)
```

For an app, NSLocalizedString is almost always the correct choice. Within a library or shared component, NSLocalizedStringFromTable should be used instead.

Localizable.strings

At runtime, NSLocalizedString determines the preferred language, and finds a corresponding Localizable.strings file in the app bundle. For example, if the user prefers French, the file fr.lproj/Localizable.strings will be consulted.

Here's what that looks like:

```
/* No comment provided by engineer. */
"Username"="nom d'utilisateur";

/* {User First Name}'s Profile */
"%@'s Profile"="profil d'%1$@";
```

Localizable.strings files are initially generated with genstrings.

The genstrings utility creates a .strings file based on whatever C or Objective-C (.c or .m) source code files are passed as the argument.

genstrings goes through each of the selected source files, and for each use of NSLocalizedString, appends the key and comment into a target file. It's up to the developer to then create a copy of that file for each targeted locale and have a translator localize it.

No Madlibs

After reading that part about localized format strings, one may be tempted to take a clever, DRY approach by creating reusable grammar templates like `@"{Noun} {Verb} {Noun}"`, and localizing each word individually...

DON'T. This cannot be stressed enough: *don't subdivide localized strings.* Context will be lost, grammatical constructions will be awkward and unidiomatic, verbs will be incorrectly conjugated, and you'll have missed the point entirely—taking great effort to make something worse than if you hadn't bothered in the first place.

For additional guidelines, see Localizing String Resources from Apple's Internationalization Programming guide.

NSLocalizedString is a remarkably reliable indicator of code quality. Those who care enough to take a few extra seconds to internationalize are very likely to be just as thoughtful when it comes to design and implementation.

Always wrap user-facing strings with NSLocalizedString.

Even if you don't plan to localize your app into any other languages, there is immense utility in being able to easily review all of the strings that a user will see.

And if localization is in the cards, it's significantly easier to NSLocalize your strings as you go along the first time, then try to find all of them after-the-fact.

UIAccessibility

iPhones and iPads—magical as they are—become downright *life-changing* for individuals with disabilities (and their families) because of Apple's commitment to accessibility.

Look no further than the WWDC 2012 Introduction Video, which opens with a blind man who walks the woods of Germany with the aid of a GPS app. It's a lovely reminder of the kind of impact our work can have on others.

Accessibility, like internationalization, is one of those topics that's difficult to get developers excited about.

UIAccessibility is an informal protocol in UIKit that provides accessibility information for user interface elements. This information is used by VoiceOver and other assistive technologies to help users with disabilities interact with your application.

All of the standard views and controls in UIKit implement UIAccessibility, so applications are nearly accessible by default. As a result, the task of improving the accessibility of an application is one of minor adjustments rather than wholesale re-implementation.

Here's a list of all of the properties in UIAccessibility:

- accessibilityLabel
- accessibilityHint
- accessibilityValue
- accessibilityLanguage
- accessibilityTraits
- accessibilityFrame
- accessibilityActivationPoint
- accessibilityElementsHidden
- accessibilityViewIsModal

Enabling Accessibility

Before going any further, take a couple minutes to play with VoiceOver, and understand how accessibility information is conveyed to the user. Open the Settings app, tap General, scroll to the bottom and tap Accessibility. In Accessibility, you'll see settings for assistive technologies grouped by category: Vision, Hearing, Learning, and Physical & Motor.

Tap VoiceOver, and then tap the VoiceOver switch to turn it on. Dismiss the alert that pops up, and VoiceOver will now be enabled on your device.

Unlike setting your device to another language, there's no real risk of not being able to figure out how to turn VoiceOver off.

Using the device in VoiceOver mode is a bit different than one might be used to:

- Tap once to select an item
- Double-Tap to activate the selected item
- Swipe with three fingers to scroll

Press the Home button and start exploring!

All of the stock Apple apps—Messages, Calendar, Weather— is fully usable in VoiceOver mode. Heck, even Camera is accessible, with the system telling you about faces detected in the camera's viewport!

By contrast (perhaps), try some 3rd-party apps from the App Store. However disappointing, some of the most visually-stunning apps, with all of their custom controls and interactions, are completely unusable in this mode.

With a clear idea of what we're working with, let's talk about implementation:

Label & Hint

The most immediate and straightforward way to improve the accessibility of an app is to ensure that each usable element has a reasonable accessibility label.

Accessibility labels and hints tell VoiceOver what to say when selecting user interface elements. This information should be helpful, yet concise.

- accessibilityLabel identifies a user interface element. Every accessible view and control must supply a label.

- accessibilityHint describes the results of interacting with a user interface element. A hint should be supplied only if the result of an interaction is not obvious from the element's label.

The Accessibility Programming Guide provides the following guidelines for labels and hints:

Guidelines for Creating Labels

If you provide a custom control or view, or if you display a custom icon in a standard control or view, you need to provide a label that:

- Very briefly describes the element. Ideally, the label consists of a single word, such as Add, Play, Delete, Search, Favorites, or Volume.

- Does not include the type of the control or view. The type information is contained in the traits attribute of the element and should never be repeated in the label.

- Begins with a capitalized word. This helps VoiceOver read the label with the appropriate inflection.

- Does not end with a period. The label is not a sentence and therefore should not end with a period.

- Is localized. Be sure to make your application available to as wide an audience as possible by localizing all strings, including accessibility attribute strings. In general, VoiceOver speaks in the language that the user specifies in International settings.

Guidelines for Creating Hints

The hint attribute describes the results of performing an action on a control or view. You should provide a hint only when the results of an action are not obvious from the element's label.

- Very briefly describes the results. Even though few controls and views need hints, strive to make the hints you do need to provide as brief as possible. Doing so decreases the amount of time users must spend listening before they can use the element.

- Begins with a verb and omits the subject. Be sure to use the third-person singular declarative form of a verb, such as "Plays," and not the imperative, such as "Play." You want to avoid using the imperative, because using it can make the hint sound like a command.

- Begins with a capitalized word and ends with a period. Even though a hint is a phrase, not a sentence, ending the hint with a period helps VoiceOver speak it with the appropriate inflection.

- Does not include the name of the action or gesture. A hint does not tell users how to perform the action, it tells users what will happen when that action occurs.

- Does not include the name of the control or view. The user gets this information from the label attribute, so you should not repeat it in the hint.

- Is localized. As with accessibility labels, hints should be available in the user's preferred language.

Traits

For custom controls, or creative re-purposing of standard controls, one should ensure that the correct accessibility traits are specified.

Accessibility traits describe a set of traits that characterize how a control behaves or should be treated.

These include distinctions like:

- Button
- Link
- Search Field
- Keyboard Key
- Static Text
- Image
- Plays Sound
- Selected

- Summary Element

- Updates Frequently

- Causes Page Turn

- Not Enabled

The accessibilityTraits property takes a bitmask of UIAccessibilityTraits values.

For example, if a custom button control displays an image and plays a sound when tapped, one should define the traits for "Button", "Image", and "Plays Sound". Or, if one were to use a UISlider for purely decorative purposes, the "Not Enabled" trait should be specified.

Frame & Activation Point

As a general rule, the cleverness of a custom UI element is directly proportional to how gnarly its implementation is. Overlapping & invisible views, table view hacks, first responder shenanigans: sometimes it's better not to ask how something works.

However, when it comes to accessibility, it's important to set the record straight.

accessibilityFrame and accessibilityActivationPoint are used to define the accessible portions and locations of UI elements, without changing their outward appearance.

As you try out your app in VoiceOver mode, try interacting with all of the elements on each screen. If the selection target is not what you expected, you can use accessibilityFrame and accessibilityActivationPoint to adjust accordingly.

Value

Accessibility value corresponds to the content of a user interface element. For a label, the value is its text. For a UISlider, it's the current numeric value represented by the control.

Want to know a quick way to improve the accessibility of table views? Try setting the accessibilityValue property for cells to be a localized summary of the cell's content. For example, for a table view that shows status updates, one might set the accessibilityLabel to "Update from #{User Name}", and the accessibilityValue to the content of that status update.

Apple has done a great service to humanity in making accessibility a first-class citizen in its hardware and software.

You're really missing out on some of the best engineering, design, and technical writing that Apple has ever done if you ignore UIAccessibility. Do yourself a favor and read the Accessibility Programming Guide for iOS.

Who knows? You may end up changing someone's life because of it.

NSFormatter

Conversion is the tireless errand of software development. Most programming tasks boil down to some variation of transforming data into something more useful.

In the case of user-facing software, converting data into human-readable form is an essential task, and a complex one at that. A user's preferred language, locale, calendar, or currency can all factor into how information should be displayed. So can other constraints, like a label's dimensions or location on the screen.

All of this is to say that sending -description to an object just isn't going to cut it in most circumstances. Even +stringWithFormat: is ultimately going to disappoint. No, the real tool for this job is NSFormatter.

NSFormatter is an abstract class for transforming data into a textual representation. It can also interpret valid textual representations back into data.

Its origins trace back to NSCell, which is used to display information and accept user input from tables, form fields, and other AppKit views. Much of the API design of NSFormatter reflects this.

Foundation provides three concrete subclasses for NSFormatter: NSNumberFormatter, NSDateFormatter, and NSByteCountFormatter. As some of the oldest members of the Foundation framework, these classes are astonishingly well-suited to their respective domains, in that way only decade-old software can.

NSNumberFormatter

NSNumberFormatter handles every aspect of number formatting imaginable, from mathematical and scientific notation, to currencies and percentages. Nearly everything about the formatter can be customized, whether its the grouping separator, currency symbol, number of significant digits, rounding behavior, fractions, character for infinity, string representation for 0, or maximum / minimum values. It can even write out numbers in several languages!

Number Styles

When using an NSNumberFormatter, the first order of business is to determine what kind of information its displaying. Is it a price? Is this a whole number, or should decimal values be shown?

NSNumberFormatter can be configured for any one of the following formats, with -setNumberStyle::

To illustrate the differences between each style, here is how the number 12345.6789 would be displayed for each:

- NSNumberFormatterNoStyle: 12346
- NSNumberFormatterDecimalStyle: 12345.6789
- NSNumberFormatterCurrencyStyle: $12345.68
- NSNumberFormatterPercentStyle: 1234567%
- NSNumberFormatterScientificStyle: 1.23456789E4
- NSNumberFormatterSpellOutStyle: twelve thousand three hundred forty-five point six seven eight nine

Locale Awareness

By default, NSNumberFormatter will format according to the current locale settings, like for currency symbol ($, £, €, etc.) or whether to use "," or "." as the decimal separator.

```
NSNumberFormatter *numberFormatter =
  [[NSNumberFormatter alloc] init];
[numberFormatter setNumberStyle:
  NSNumberFormatterCurrencyStyle];

for (NSString *identifier in @[@"en_US", @"fr_FR"]) {
    numberFormatter.locale =
        [NSLocale localeWithLocaleIdentifier:identifier];
    NSLog(@"%@: %@", identifier,
        [numberFormatter stringFromNumber:@(1234.5678)]);
}
```

en_US	$ 1234.57
fr_FR	1 234,57 €

All of those settings can be overridden on an individual basis,
but for most apps, the best strategy would be deferring to the
locale's default settings.

Rounding & Significant Digits

In order to prevent numbers from getting annoyingly
pedantic *("thirty-two point three three, repeating, of
course...")*, make sure get a handle on NSNumberFormatter's
rounding behavior.

The easiest way to do this, would be to do
setUsesSignificantDigits: to YES, and then set minimum and
maximum number of significant digits appropriately. For
example, a number formatter used for approximate distances

in directions, would do well with significant digits to the tenths place for miles or kilometers, but only the ones place for feet or meters.

For anything more advanced, an NSDecimalNumberHandler object can be set as the roundingBehavior property of a number formatter.

NSDateFormatter

NSDateFormatter is the be all and end all of getting textual representations of both dates and times.

Date & Time Styles

The most important properties for a NSDateFormatter object is its dateStyle and timeStyle. Like NSNumberFormatter - numberStyle, these properties provide common preset configurations for common formats. In this case, the formats are distinguished by their specificity (more specific ⇒ longer).

Both properties share a single set of enum values:

Style	Description	Examples	
		Date	Time
NSDateFormatter NoStyle	Specifies no style.		
NSDateFormatter ShortStyle	Specifies a short style, typically numeric only.	11/23/37	3:30pm
NSDateFormatter MediumStyle	Specifies a medium style, typically with abbreviated text.	Nov 23, 1937	3:30:32pm
NSDateFormatter LongStyle	Specifies a long style, typically with full text.	November 23, 1937	3:30:32pm
NSDateFormatter FullStyle	Specifies a full style with complete details.	Tuesday, April 12, 1952 AD	3:30:42pm PST

dateStyle and timeStyle are set independently. For example, to display just the time, an NSDateFormatter would be configured with a dateStyle of NSDateFormatterNoStyle:

```
NSDateFormatter *formatter =
   [[NSDateFormatter alloc] init];
[formatter setDateStyle:NSDateFormatterNoStyle];
[formatter setTimeStyle:NSDateFormatterMediumStyle];
NSLog(@"%@", [formatter stringFromDate:[NSDate date]]);
// 12:11:19pm
```

Whereas setting both to NSDateFormatterLongStyle yields the following:

```
NSDateFormatter *formatter =
  [[NSDateFormatter alloc] init];
[formatter setDateStyle:NSDateFormatterLongStyle];
[formatter setTimeStyle:NSDateFormatterLongStyle];
NSLog(@"%@", [formatter stringFromDate:[NSDate date]]);
// Monday, November 11, 2013 12:11:19pm PST
```

As one might expect, each aspect of the date format can alternatively be configured individually, a la carte. For any aspiring time wizards NSDateFormatter has a bevy of different knobs and switches to play with.

Relative Formatting

As of iOS 4 / OS X 10.6, NSDateFormatter supports relative date formatting for certain locales with the doesRelativeDateFormatting property. Setting this to YES would format the date of [NSDate date] to "Today".

Re-Using Formatter Instances

Perhaps the most critical detail to keep in mind when using formatters is that they are extremely expensive to create. Even just an alloc init of an NSNumberFormatter within a tight loop is enough to bring an app to its knees.

Therefore, it's strongly recommended that formatters be created once, and re-used as much as possible.

If it's just a single method using a particular formatter, a static instance is a good strategy:

```objc
- (void)fooWithNumber:(NSNumber *)number {
    static NSNumberFormatter *_formatter = nil;
    static dispatch_once_t onceToken;
    dispatch_once(&onceToken, ^{
        _formatter = [[NSNumberFormatter alloc] init];
        [_formatter setNumberStyle:
            NSNumberFormatterDecimalStyle];
    });

    NSString *string =
      [_formatter stringFromNumber:number];

    // ...
}
```

dispatch_once guarantees that the specified block is called only the first time it's encountered.

If the formatter is used across several methods in the same class, that static instance can be refactored into a singleton method:

```
+ (NSNumberFormatter *)numberFormatter {
    static NSNumberFormatter *_formatter = nil;
    static dispatch_once_t onceToken;
    dispatch_once(&onceToken, ^{
        _formatter = [[NSNumberFormatter alloc] init];
        [_formatter setNumberStyle:
          NSNumberFormatterDecimalStyle];
    });

    return _formatter;
}
```

If the same formatter is privately implemented across several classes, one could either expose it publicly in one of the classes, or implement the singleton method in a category on NSNumberFormatter.

Presenting useful information to users is as much about content as presentation. Invest in learning all of the secrets of NSFormatter to get every detail exactly how you want them.

And if you find yourself with formatting logic scattered across your app, consider creating your own NSFormatter subclass to consolidate all of that business logic in one place.

CFStringTransform

Everything you ever need to know about how nice a language is to use can be determined by two indicators:

1. API Consistency

2. Quality of String Implementation

NSString is the crown jewel of Foundation. In an age where other languages still struggle to handle Unicode correctly, NSString can not only handle anything you throw at it, but it can turn around and parse that input into linguistic tags. It's unfairly good.

But as powerful as NSString / NSMutableString are, one would be remiss not to mention their toll-free bridged cousin, CFMutableString. Or more specifically, CFStringTransform.

As denoted by the CF prefix, CFStringTransform is part of Core Foundation, making it a C, rather than Objective-C API. The function returns a Boolean for whether or not the transform was successful, and takes the following arguments:

- string: The string to be transformed. Since this argument is a CFMutableStringRef, an NSMutableString can be passed using toll-free bridging.

- range: The range of the string over which the transformation should be applied. Pass NULL for the transformation to be applied over the entire string.

- transform: The ICU transform to apply.

- reverse: Whether to run the transform in reverse, where applicable.

CFStringTransform covers a lot of ground with its transform argument. Here's a rundown of what it can do:

Stripping Accents and Diacritics

Énġlišh långuāge läcks iñterêßţing diaçrïtičş, so it can be useful to normalize extended Latin characters into ASCII-friendly representations. Get rid of the squiggly bits using the kCFStringTransformStripCombiningMarks transform.

Naming Unicode Characters

kCFStringTransformToUnicodeName allows one to finally determine the Unicode standard name for special characters, including Emoji. For instance, "🐷" becomes "{PIG FACE}".

Transliterating Between Orthographies

With the exception of English (with its complicated spelling inconsistencies), writing systems encode speech sounds into phonetic, written representations. European languages generally use the Latin alphabet (with a few added diacritics), Russian uses Cyrillic, Japanese uses Hiragana & Katakana, and Thai, Korean, & Arabic each have their own scripts.

Although each language has a particular inventory of sounds that other languages may not have, the overlap across all of the major writing systems is remarkably high—enough so that one can rather effectively transliterate from one to another.

CFStringTransform can transliterate between Latin and Arabic, Cyrillic, Greek, Korean (Hangul), Hebrew, Japanese (Hiragana & Katakana), Mandarin Chinese, and Thai. And not only that, but those transformations are all reversible:

Transformation	Input	Output
kCFStringTransformLatinArabic	mrḥbạ	مرحبا
kCFStringTransformLatinCyrillic	privet	привет
kCFStringTransformLatinGreek	geiá sou	γειά σου
kCFStringTransformLatinHangul	annyeonghaseyo	안녕하세요
kCFStringTransformLatinHebrew	şlwm	שלום
kCFStringTransformLatinHiragana	hiragana	ひらがな
kCFStringTransformLatinKatakana	katakana	カタカナ
kCFStringTransformLatinThai	s̄wạs̄dī	สวัสดี
kCFStringTransform HiraganaKatakana	にほんご	ニホンゴ
kCFStringTransformMandarinLatin	中文	zhōng wén

Normalize User-Generated Content

One of the more practical applications for all of this is to normalize unpredictable user input. Even if an application doesn't specifically deal with languages, it should be able to intelligently process anything the user types.

For example, to build a searchable index of greetings from around the world, one could do the following:

First, apply the kCFStringTransformToLatin transform to transliterate all non-English text into a phonetic Latin alphabetic representation.

```
Hello! こんにちは! สวัสดี! مرحبا! 您好! →
Hello! kon'nichiha! s̆wạs̆dī! mrḥbạ! nín hǎo!
```

Next, apply the kCFStringTransformStripCombiningMarks transform to remove any diacritics or accents.

```
Hello! kon'nichiha! swasdi! mrhba! nin hao!
```

Finally, downcase the text and use CFStringTokenizer to split the text into tokens, and index on them.

```
(hello, kon'nichiha, swasdi, mrhba, nin, hao)
```

Doing the same to search text entered by the user allows for content to be searched phonetically, regardless of either the language of the search string or the content.

CFStringTransform is an insanely powerful way to bend language to your will. And it's but one of many powerful APIs that await you if you're brave enough to explore outside of Objective-C's warm OO embrace.

NSLinguisticTagger

NSLinguisticTagger is a veritable Swiss Army Knife of linguistic functionality, with the ability to tokenize natural language strings into words, determine their part-of-speech & stem, extract names of people, places, & organizations, and determine the languages & respective writing system.

For most developers, this is far more power than anyone knows what to do with. But perhaps this is just for lack sufficient opportunity to try. After all, almost every application deals with natural language in one way or another... perhaps NSLinguisticTagger could add a new level of polish, or enable brand new features entirely.

Introduced with iOS 5, NSLinguisticTagger is a contemporary to Siri, raising speculation that it was a byproduct of the personal assistant's development.

Consider a typical question one might ask Siri:

What is the weather in San Francisco?

Computers are a long ways off from "understanding" this question literally, but with a few simple tricks, they can do a reasonable job determining the intention of the question with to reasonable degree of confidence:

```
NSString *question =
  @"What is the weather in San Francisco?";
NSLinguisticTaggerOptions options =
  NSLinguisticTaggerOmitWhitespace  |
  NSLinguisticTaggerOmitPunctuation |
  NSLinguisticTaggerJoinNames;

NSLinguisticTagger *tagger =
  [[NSLinguisticTagger alloc] initWithTagSchemes:
    [NSLinguisticTagger
      availableTagSchemesForLanguage:@"en"]
                                 options:options];
tagger.string = question;

NSRange range = NSMakeRange(0, [question length])
[tagger enumerateTagsInRange: range
    scheme:NSLinguisticTagSchemeNameTypeOrLexicalClass
              options:options
              usingBlock:
^(NSString *tag, NSRange tokenRange, NSRange, BOOL *) {
    NSString *token =
      [question substringWithRange:tokenRange];
    NSLog(@"%@: %@", token, tag);
}];
```

This code would print the following:

```
What: Pronoun
is: Verb
the: Determiner
weather: Noun
in: Preposition
San Francisco: PlaceName
```

Filtering on nouns, verbs, and place name, yields:

```
[is, weather, San Francisco]
```

Based on this (perhaps in conjunction with something like the Latent Semantic Mapping framework) an app can conclude that a reasonable course of action would be making an API request to determine the current weather conditions in the city of San Francisco.

Tagging Schemes

NSLinguisticTagger can be configured to tag different kinds of information by specifying any of the following tagging schemes:

*   NSLinguisticTagSchemeTokenType: Classifies tokens according to their broad type: word, punctuation, whitespace, etc.

- NSLinguisticTagSchemeLexicalClass: Classifies tokens according to class: part of speech for words, type of punctuation or whitespace, etc.

- NSLinguisticTagSchemeNameType: Classifies tokens as to whether they are part of named entities of various types or not.

- NSLinguisticTagSchemeNameTypeOrLexicalClass: Follows NSLinguisticTagSchemeNameType for names, and NSLinguisticTagSchemeLexicalClass for all other tokens.

Here's a list of the various token types associated with each scheme:

NSLinguisticTagSchemeNameTypeOrLexicalClass, as the name suggests, is the union between NSLinguisticTagSchemeNameType & NSLinguisticTagSchemeLexicalClass

---

NSLinguisticTagSchemeTokenType

NSLinguisticTagWord
NSLinguisticTagPunctuation
NSLinguisticTagWhitespace
NSLinguisticTagOther

NSLinguisticTagSchemeLexicalClass

NSLinguisticTagNoun
NSLinguisticTagVerb
NSLinguisticTagAdjective
NSLinguisticTagAdverb
NSLinguisticTagPronoun
NSLinguisticTagDeterminer
NSLinguisticTagParticle
NSLinguisticTagPreposition
NSLinguisticTagNumber
NSLinguisticTagConjunction
NSLinguisticTagInterjection
NSLinguisticTagClassifier
NSLinguisticTagIdiom
NSLinguisticTagOtherWord
NSLinguisticTagSentenceTerminator
NSLinguisticTagOpenQuote
NSLinguisticTagCloseQuote
NSLinguisticTagOpenParenthesis
NSLinguisticTagCloseParenthesis
NSLinguisticTagWordJoiner
NSLinguisticTagDash
NSLinguisticTagOtherPunctuation
NSLinguisticTagParagraphBreak
NSLinguisticTagOtherWhitespace

NSLinguisticTagSchemeNameType

NSLinguisticTagPersonalName
NSLinguisticTagPlaceName
NSLinguisticTagOrganizationName

For basic tokenization, use NSLinguisticTagSchemeTokenType, which will distinguishes between words and whitespace or punctuation.

For information like part-of-speech, go with NSLinguisticTagSchemeLexicalClass.

Continuing with the tagging schemes:

- NSLinguisticTagSchemeLemma: This tag scheme supplies a stem forms of the words, if known.

- NSLinguisticTagSchemeLanguage: Tags tokens according to their script. The tag values will be standard language abbreviations such as "en", "fr", "de", etc., as used with the NSOrthography class. Note that the tagger generally attempts to determine the language of text at the level of an entire sentence or paragraph, rather than word by word.

- NSLinguisticTagSchemeScript: Tags tokens according to their script. The tag values will be standard script abbreviations such as "Latn", "Cyrl", "Jpan", "Hans", "Hant", etc.

As demonstrated in the example above, first initialize an NSLinguisticTagger with an array of all of the different schemes that you wish to use, specify the input string, and enumerate each of the tags.

Tagging Options

In addition to the available tagging schemes, there are several options that can be passed to NSLinguisticTagger (combined with bitwise OR, |) to slightly change its behavior:

- NSLinguisticTaggerOmitWords
- NSLinguisticTaggerOmitPunctuation
- NSLinguisticTaggerOmitWhitespace
- NSLinguisticTaggerOmitOther

Each of these options omit the broad categories of tags described. For example, NSLinguisticTagSchemeLexicalClass, which would otherwise distinguish between different kinds of punctuation, would have all of those ignored with NSLinguisticTaggerOmitPunctuation. This is preferable to manually filtering these tag types in enumeration blocks or with predicates.

The last option is specific to NSLinguisticTagSchemeNameType:

- NSLinguisticTaggerJoinNames

By default, each token in a name is treated separately. In many circumstances, it makes sense to treat names like "San Francisco" as a single token, rather than two. Passing this option makes it so.

Natural language is under-utilized in user interface design—especially on mobile devices. When implemented effectively, a single utterance from the user can achieve the equivalent of a handful of touch interactions, in a fraction of the time.

It's not easy, but if we spent a fraction of the time we use to make our visual interfaces pixel-perfect, we could completely re-imagine how users interact with apps and devices. And with NSLinguisticTagger, it's never been easier to get started.

API Design

The Law of Demeter

Information is power.
Power corrupts.
Good fences make good neighbors.

Also known as the "principle of least knowledge", The Law of Demeter is a design guideline that advocates for functionality to be loosely coupled across a system. Essentially: objects are best when they know least about one another.

Limiting the number of incoming & outgoing connections between components in a system is the only viable strategy for managing complexity as an application scales.

Everything should be ruthlessly modularized.

Central to this design philosophy is the practice of "information hiding". By playing things close to the vest, a developer affords themselves the flexibility to change implementation details later.

Languages in the C family are naturally aligned with this philosophy, because of their explicit separation of interface (.h files) from implementation (.c / .cpp / .m / .mm / .cs files).

Files #import the headers of other files they want to interact with, but are limited to seeing only the methods, functions, and constants exposed in those headers. Anything could be going on behind the scenes... and that's sort of the point, actually. Single-responsibility objects can't be bothered to worry about how state is stored internally, or which sorting strategy is being used—it's just not in the job description.

Objective-C has a handful of unique language features that can be used to hide information. All professional developers should know them well and use them often.

Class Continuations

Class continuations, or class extensions, are anonymous categories that allow an implementation to privately re-declare parts of the original interface.

For example, to add a private property to a Person class, declare it in a class continuation before the @implementation:

Person.h

```
@interface Person
@property (nonatomic, strong) NSString *name;
@property (nonatomic, strong) NSDate *birthday;
@end
```

Person.m

```
@interface Person ()
@property (readwrite, nonatomic, strong) NSString
*gossip;
@end
```

Redeclaring readonly Properties

All properties should start out as publicly readonly, granting readwrite access only after considering how and whether a user should be able to mutate that particular aspect of state.

One common example is an object with an array-backed collection. Rather than exposing a readwrite interface or its mutable counterpart, the backing array is provided as readonly, with a method for adding a new item.

Although Objective-C lacks generics, this approach provides a workable type-safe solution to managing collections. It also provides a single code path for modifying the collection:

Order.h

```
@interface Order
@property (readonly, nonatomic, strong) NSArray *items;

- (void)addItem:(Item *)item;
```

Order.m

```
@interface Order ()
@property (readwrite, nonatomic, strong) NSArray *items;
@end

@implementation Order
- (void)addItem:(Item *)item {
  self.items = [self.items arrayByAddingObject:item];
}
@end
```

A variation of this approach has an NSMutableArray mutableItems readwrite property in the implementation that is @synthesize'd in place of the readonly items property.

extern & static

Constant variables should not publicly expose their values. This is for the safety of both API provider and consumer.

Revealing a magic constant can tempt users to pass the literal value in place of the reference. Keeping the value secret allows that value change in subsequent releases without breaking any code that references the constant.

The same goes for functions, whose implementation details would be out of place in the interface, though more for reasons of clutter rather than security.

Only variables or functions make sense to be shared should be declared extern in the interface. All internal or private members should use the static storage type in the implementation.

Post.h

```
extern NSString * const XXPublicationName;

extern NSString * XXBylineForPerson(Person *person);
```

Post.m

```objc
NSString * const XXPublicationName =
  @"NSHipster Times-Picayune"

static NSString * const XXPublicationBylineFormat =
  @"by %@";

NSString * XXBylineForPerson(Person *person) {
  return [NSString stringWithFormat:
    XXPublicationBylineFormat, person.name];
}
```

Delegates & Protocols

No part of an app should require special knowledge of any other part of the app in order to make things work.

Consider a table view that displays a list of posts, with a + button in the navigation bar, which presents a modal for creating a new post. Once the form is submitted, the modal is dismissed and the new post is added to the list.

Anti-Patterns

- On submit:, the form view controller creates a post and adds the post to the collection, either through a reference to the list view controller, or by introspecting its presenting view controller. This strongly couples the form to the list, when the form might be useful to other view controllers, such as one for displaying a single post.

- A notification is posted when the form is submitted, which is then listened for by the list view controller. When the notification is received, its object is added to the data source. This approach is not terrible, but notifications are more appropriate when more than one component needs to know about a particular event. A more centralized state coordinator like Core Data would be appropriate to keep track of insertions, updates, and deletes of domain objects across an application.

- The list view controller keeps a reference to a form view controller, and adds a condition to viewWillAppear: that introspects the contents of the form, and adds a post from the contents if present. This way leads to madness.

Correct Approach

The delegate pattern allows for a loose coupling between components through a protocol. In this particular case, it makes sense for EditPostViewController to be responsible for serializing fields into properties on a Post object itself.

Another thing to note is that PostsViewController conforms to EditPostViewControllerDelegate in its class extension, rather than its original @interface declaration. This helps to cut down on the semantic clutter of the public interface.

CreatePostViewController.h

```
@protocol EditPostViewControllerDelegate
- (void)viewController:(EditPostViewController
*)viewController
        didCreatePost:(Post *)post;
@end


@interface EditPostViewController : UIViewController
// ...
@end
```

PostsViewController.m

```
@interface PostsViewController () \
    <EditPostViewControllerDelegate>
@end
```

```
@implementation PostsViewController

- (IBAction)create:(id)sender {
  EditPostViewController *viewController =
[[EditPostViewController alloc] init];
  viewController.delegate = self;
  UINavigationController *navigationController =
[[UINavigationController alloc]
initWithRootViewController:viewController];

  [self presentModalViewController:navigationController
animated:YES];
}

#pragma mark - EditPostViewControllerDelegate

- (void)viewController:(EditPostViewController
*)viewController
        didCreatePost:(Post *)post
{
  self.posts = [self.posts arrayByAddingObject:post];
  [self.tableView reloadData];

  [self dismissModalViewControllerAnimated:YES];
}
@end
```

The Law of Demeter teaches us that what you don't know can't hurt you. Building your app around know-nothing components is the only way to ensure that a codebase will be able to grow and evolve over time.

Approach API design from the perspective of the consumer, and you'll find that you'll have a much better time as a consumer yourself.

The Principle of
Least Surprise

Unlike other disciplines, where a hard day's work is rewarded
with a physical manifestation of one's efforts, software is
invisible, intangible, and—in many ways—imaginary. Things
happen in a millionth of a second, on top of a dozen layers of
abstraction. By all accounts, modern software just shouldn't
be possible. The fact that any of this works is a miracle.

It's the least we can do to salvage any semblance of causality
we can muster in our own operational domain.

"The Principle of Least Surprise" describes a general approach
to software that celebrates sanity over cleverness: clear intent,
reasonable defaults, and providing a sense of control to the
developer.

Side Effects & Unintended Consequences

State is the enemy of logical consistency. To mix idiomatic
metaphors, it's the wrench in the machine that gums up the

works. Anything a language or framework can do to reduce or eliminate the occasions for state change, the more robust an application built on it will be.

It is therefore useful to make a distinction between methods that change state, "mutators", and those that don't, "accessors". @synthesize generates an accessor / mutator pair for @properties in the form of a getter and setter.

In most cases, accessors act as wrappers for direct ivar access. Alternatively, accessors may memoize a computed result, provide a lazily-initialized default value, or keep track of when a value is accessed, but that's about as complicated as they should get.

Mutators range in complexity from directly setting an ivar value to performing a series of destructive actions across a system. Methods that create large amounts of entropy should be wielded with caution. Remember: predictable systems are always preferable to clever ones.

For lack of language features to enforce this distinction, Objective-C must rely on conventions to communicate the difference:

- **Accessors** are named with a **Noun Phrase** (NP), *(e.g., name, attributedString)*, with the exception of methods with a BOOL return type, which can precede with is *(e.g. isDirectory)*

- **Mutators** are named with a **Verb Phrase** (VP), *(e.g. setName:, resetCache, performSelector:)*

Too Clever By Half

The mark of an "expert beginner" programmer is the desire to be clever, by invoking obscure design patterns, elaborate meta-programming, or runtime manipulations that teeter on the brink of calamity.

In reality, most programs just aren't that interesting. There's no reason to get fancy.

...but of course, everyone would like to think that they are the exception. The sooner you can start thinking of the project in front of you in terms of engineering rather than performance art, the better off you'll be as a professional.

Objective-C provides a number of avenues for creative hackery, from method swizzling and associated objects, to forward invocations and compiler directives.

Powerful, though they are, these advanced tricks should be seen as a last resort, reserved for cases when no reasonable alternative exists.

What scares the hell out of veteran programmers is code that messes with underlying system assumptions. Re-ordering internal view hierarchies? Stomping on top of private methods in subclass implementations? Swizzling a base implementation on NSObject? This is the stuff of nightmares and App Store rejections.

Good code is pretty boring on the atomic level. Don't make things too complicated for yourself (or others).

Follow the example of a bistro restaurant: simple dishes with good ingredients, well-executed. Good taste is rooted in restraint.

Naming

There are only 2 hard things in programming: naming, cache invalidation, and off-by-one-errors.

wokka wokka wokka

Names bring ideas into focus. What a programmer calls a variable, method, function, class, or even the project itself is often one of the most important decisions they make.

Good names establishes intention, informing how something should be used. They unite a codebase around a set of shared concepts. Often, the best way to reduce or eliminate bugs is to refactor how things are named (an exercise, which may reveal some faulty assumptions along the way).

What makes a good name? Well, it must be descriptive, but not overly so. It must avoid ambiguity among other similarly named modules, while being both memorable and easy to spell. A good name builds on an existing vocabulary, using known words in a way most people agree upon within the particular domain.

Naming is a subjective exercise. Each community—and indeed each project—has its own milieu of standards and conventions. What follows are guidelines representative of Objective-C code written today.

Leading By Example

Make no mistake: Objective-C is Apple's language. If you are writing Objective-C, you are almost necessarily developing on their platform. Whatever they say goes.

In practice, this has worked out pretty well for us as developers. Apple's code is, more often than not, of exceptional quality. System frameworks are remarkably well-designed, reasonably documented, and relatively self-consistent. That's not to say that Apple doesn't make mistakes, or is immune from critique, but in all fairness, they really do a great job with the technology we use everyday.

As a consequence of this opinionated, top-down leadership, the rules for naming things in Objective-C is pretty simple: follow Apple's example.

Apple summarizes their own API naming conventions as follows:

- Clarity and brevity are both important, but clarity should never be sacrificed for brevity.

- Avoid names that are ambiguous.

- Use verbs in the names of methods or functions that represent actions.

- Use prefixes for class names and for symbols associated with the class, such as functions and data types.

When designing a new class, peruse the documentation for related functionality, and take note of the patterns and conventions used in the standard frameworks. Every iOS and OS X developer is familiar with how Apple does things, so the closer one can follow their example, the easier it will be for others to get up to speed.

Design Patterns

What is perhaps most striking about Apple's naming methodologies is their usage of design patterns: MVC, delegates, target-action, observers, the responder chain, facades (viz. class clusters), enumerators, decorators, serializers... the Gang of Four is well represented in Cupertino.

It helps to call things what they are. And while Apple has taken certain, how you say, *liberties* in denoting certain design patterns, they've otherwise set an excellent example.

By thinking about problems in terms of architecture, one can arrive at a viable solution more quickly than if they were to take a bottom-up approach. Design patterns provide a common vocabulary for describing those decisions made in the design process. When appropriate, design patterns offer both clarity and brevity to names, so look for opportunities to apply them in your own code.

Names are something to agonize over. However, the strong examples found within Objective-C system frameworks provide a solid semantic precedent that makes the job easier.

Programming is the craft of conveying structured meaning through designed language, so take time to refine each word to maximum efficacy.

Community

Stewardship

Open Source communities function within what economists describe as a Gift Economy. Rather than paying one another for goods or services through barter or currency, everyone shares freely with one another, and gains social currency based on their generosity. It's similar to how friends tend to take turns inviting one another over for dinner or a party.

With the negligible cost of distributing software over the Internet, developers are able to participate with millions of others around the world. And as a result, we have been able to collaboratively build amazing software.

In terms of open source participation, releasing code is only one aspect—and arguably not even the most important one. Developing an open source project requires equal parts engineering, product design, communication, and community management. But the true deciding factor for whether an open source project succeeds is stewardship.

Stewardship is an old word. It evokes the ethic of public service and duty. To be a steward is to embody the responsibilities that come with ownership. It is an act that justifies authority through continued accountability; both the greatest challenge and reward of creating and maintaining a project.

Creating

It's not enough to dump a pile of source code somewhere and declare it "open source". To do so misses the point entirely. The first step of stewardship is to clearly explain the goal and value proposition of the project, and establish clear expectations going forward.

README

A README is the most important part of any open source project. It describes why someone would want to use the code, and how they may start to do so.

All good READMEs have the following:

- A short, one or two sentence introduction that clearly explains what the project is in simple, understandable language.

- A section describing the basic usage of the primary tasks of the project. For example, a UI component would provide sample code of how to create, configure, and add itself to a view.

- A list of requirements and instructions on how to install the code into one's own project.

- Links to documentation and resources for additional information.

- Contact information for the author or current maintainer.

- A quick statement about the licensing terms of the project.

LICENSE

All open source code should be released under an appropriate license. Unless you have a really good reason not to, choose from any of the licenses approved by the Open Source Initiative, like MIT, Apache 2.0, or GPL.

If you're unsure which license to choose, there are several resources online that you can use to learn more. Most open source Objective-C projects are released under an MIT license, which is known to be compatible with the terms of distribution for the App Store.

Screenshot

For projects with any kind of user interface, such as a custom control, view, or animation, posting a screenshot should be considered a requirement.

Buying anything "sight unseen" is a bad idea, and the same goes for consumers of open source. Although there are no monetary costs involved, evaluating a project requires a nontrivial investment in time and energy. A screenshot helps potential consumers decide if your code is worth checking out.

Demo

Actions speak louder than words. And no matter how comprehensive a README file is, any open source project can be improved with a working example.

There's just something about seeing the code in a real context that allows developers to grok what's going on. It's also nice to have a starting point for tinkering around.

At the very least, an example can be used to bootstrap the process of fixing bugs or developing new features, both for you and for anyone who wants to contribute. It's also a great place to incorporate any testing infrastructure for the project.

Distribution

One of the great developments in the Objective-C open source community—and in many ways, what has allowed it to flourish as it has recently—is CocoaPods.

CocoaPods is the de facto dependency manager for integrating third party code in iOS and Mac OS X projects. At this point, it's pretty much expected that any library worth using salt is distributed with a .podspec:

NSHipsterKit.podspec

```
Pod::Spec.new do |s|
  s.name     = 'NSHipsterKit'
  s.version  = '1.0.0'
  s.license  = 'MIT'
  s.summary  = "A pretty obscure library.
                You've probably never heard of it."
  s.homepage = 'http://nshipster.com'
  s.authors  = { 'Mattt Thompson' =>
                 'mattt@nshipster.com' }
  s.source   = { :git => 'https://github.com/nshipster/
NSHipsterKit.git', :tag => '1.0.0' }
  s.source_files = 'NSHipsterKit'
end
```

Once the .podspec has been submitted to the CocoaPods specs repository, a consumer would be able to add it to their own project with a Podfile:

Podfile

```
platform :ios, '7.0'
pod 'NSHipsterKit', '~> 1.0'
```

Maintaining

Once the initial thrill of releasing a library has passed, the real work begins. The thing to remember is that a flurry of stars, watchers, and tweets may be exciting, but they don't amount to anything of real importance. Only when users start to come with their questions, issues, and pull requests does code become software.

Versioning

Versioning is a contract that library authors make to consumers in how software will be changed over time.

The prevailing convention is Semantic Versioning, in which a release has a major, minor, and patch version, with each level signifying particular usage implications.

- A patch, or bugfix, release changes only implementation, keeping the public API and thus all documented intact. Consumers should be able to update between patch versions without any change to their own code.

- A minor, or point, release changes the public API in non-breaking ways, such as adding a new feature. Again, developers should expect to have consumer code between minor versions work pretty much as expected.

- A major release is anything that changes the public API in a backwards-incompatible way. Updating between major versions effectively means migrating consumer code to a new library.

A comprehensive set of guidelines for semantic versioning can be found at http://semver.org

---

By following a few basic rules for versioning, developers are able to set clear expectations for how changes affect will affect shipping code.

Deviating from these conventions as an author is disrespectful to anyone using the software, so take this responsibility seriously.

Answering Questions

One of our greatest flaws as humans is our relative inability to comprehend not knowing or understanding something that we ourselves do. This makes is extremely difficult to diagnose (and at times empathize with) misunderstandings that someone else might be having.

There's also a slight sadistic tendency for developers to lord knowledge over anyone who doesn't know as much as they do. *We* had to figure it out for ourselves (uphill both ways, in the snow) so why shouldn't *they* have to as well?

We must learn how to do better than this. RTFM is a lame answer to any question. It's also a dead-end to a potential learning experience for yourself.

Rather than disdaining questions, take them as an opportunity to understand what you can do better. Each question is a data point for what could be clarified or improved within your own software and documentation. And one thing to consider: for each person who asks a question, there are dozens of others who don't and get frustrated and give up. Answering one question on a mailing list or developer forum helps many more people than just the asker.

Transitioning

The fate of any successful enterprise is to outgrow its original creators. While this may be a troubling or unwelcome notion, it is nevertheless something that any responsible creator should keep in mind.

If anything, the reminder that all of this is fleeting gives reason to find enjoyment in even the minutia of a preoccupation.

Recruiting & Delegating

As a project grows, natural leaders will emerge. If you see someone consistently answering questions in issues or sending pull requests with bug fixes, ask if they would like some more responsibility.

Co-maintainers don't come pre-baked; individuals must grow into that role. And that role is something that must be defined over time by everyone involved. Avoid drama and hard feelings by communicating honestly and often with collaborators.

Sunsetting

All software has a lifecycle. At some point, all things must come to an end. Libraries outgrow their usefulness, or supplanted by another piece of software, or simply fall out of favor.

In any case, there will come a time when the lights need to be turned off, and it is the responsibility of the maintainer to wrap things up.

- Announce the ending of the project, offering suggestions for how to migrate to another solution.

- Keep the project around, but make a commit that removes source files from the master branch.
  (Git will keep everything safe in history)

- Thank everyone involved for their help and contributions.

The alternative is to become a liability, an attractive nuisance... a mockery of what once was a respectable code base.

Creating is one of the most fulfilling experiences in life, and it's something that's only improved by sharing with others. As software developers, we have a unique opportunity to be unbounded by physical limitations to help one another.

On the occasion that you do have the opportunity to participate in the community, be sure to make the most of it— you'll be happy you did.

Empathy

Great software is created to scratch one's own itch. Being close to a problem provides not only insight for how to solve it, but the motivation to actually follow through.

It's the better angels of our nature that compel us to share these solutions with one other. And in the open source world, we do so freely, with only a karmic expectation of paying the favor forward.

We naturally want to help one another, to explain ideas, to be generous and patient. However, on the Internet, human nature seems to drop a few packets. Practicing empathy online becomes a feat of moral athleticism. Lacking many of the faculties to humanize and understand one another (facial expressions, voice tonality, non-verbal cues) we can lose sight of who we're talking to, and become less human ourselves.

Before engaging with someone, take a moment to visualize how that encounter would play out in real life. Would you be proud of how you conducted yourself?

Rather than responding defensively to snark or aggression, stop to consider what could have motivated that reaction. Is there something you could be doing better as a programmer or community member? Or are they just having a bad day? (We've all had our bad days).

And let it never be that someone is marginalized for their ability to communicate in English. Be patient and ask questions. Respond simply and clearly.

Everything you need to succeed as a software developer extends from a conscious practice of empathy.

About NSHipster

NSHipster is a journal of the overlooked bits in Objective-C and Cocoa. Updated weekly.

Launched in the Summer of 2012, NSHipster has become an essential resource for iOS and Mac developers around the world.

Colophon

The text is set in Minion, by Robert Slimbach, with code excerpts set in Menlo, by Jim Lyles.

The cover is set in Trajan by Carol Twombly, in an homage to *The C Programming Language* by Brian Kernighan and Dennis Ritchie.

About the Author

 Mattt Thompson is the creator & maintainer of AFNetworking and other popular open-source projects, including Postgres.app, Induction, Helios, and Nomad.

Previously, Mattt has worked as Mobile Lead at Heroku, an iPhone & iPad Developer at Gowalla, and a Rails and Front-End Engineer at Cerego.

His work has taken him across the United States and around the world, to speak at conferences and meetups about topics in Objective-C, Ruby, Javascript, web development, design, linguistics, and philosophy.

Mattt holds a Bachelor's degree in Philosophy and Linguistics from Carnegie Mellon University.

Made in the USA
Charleston, SC
01 December 2013